THE
MIGHTY CHIEFTAINS

✚

This volume is one of a series that chronicles the history and culture of the Native Americans. Other books in the series include:

The Cover: Rain in the Face, a Hunkpapa Sioux reputed to have killed Custer at the Battle of Little Bighorn in 1876, achieved the rank of war chief through acts of valor. He earned his name as a teenager during a fight with Gros Ventre warriors when rain smeared his red and black face paint.

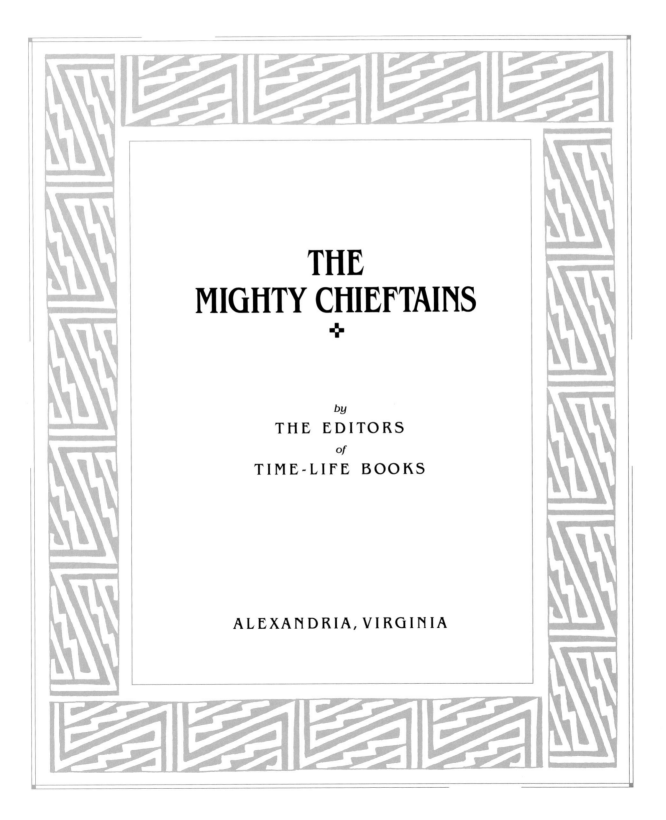

THE MIGHTY CHIEFTAINS

✛

by
THE EDITORS
of
TIME-LIFE BOOKS

ALEXANDRIA, VIRGINIA

THE AMERICAN INDIANS

SERIES EDITOR: Henry Woodhead
Administrative Editor: Jane Edwin

Editorial Staff for *The Mighty Chieftains*
Senior Art Directors: Ray Ripper (principal),
Dale Pollekoff
Picture Editor: Susan V. Kelly
Text Editors: John Newton (principal),
Stephen G. Hyslop
Writers: Maggie Debelius, Stephanie Lewis
Associate Editors/Research: Harris J. Andrews,
Mary Helena McCarthy (principals), Kirk E. Denkler,
Quentin Gaines Story, Marilyn Murphy Terrell
Assistant Art Director: Susan M. Gibas
Senior Copyeditor: Ann Lee Bruen
Picture Coordinator: David C. Beard
Editorial Assistant: Gemma Villanueva

Special Contributors: Amy Aldrich, George Constable,
George G. Daniels, Susan Perry, Peter Pocock, Lydia
Preston, David S. Thomson (text); Martha Lee
Beckington, Barbara Fleming, Jennifer Veech
(research); Barbara L. Klein (index).

Correspondents: Elisabeth Kraemer-Singh (Bonn),
Christine Hinze (London), Christina Lieberman
(New York), Maria Vincenza Aloisi (Paris), Ann
Natanson (Rome). Valuable assistance was also
provided by: Corky Bastlund (Copenhagen), Robert
Kroon (Geneva), Trini Bandrés (Madrid), Elizabeth
Brown, Katheryn White (New York), Carolyn Sackett
(Seattle).

Library of Congress Cataloging in Publication Data
The mighty chieftains/by the editors of Time-
Life Books.
    p. cm.
    Includes bibliographical references and index.
    ISBN 0-8094-9429-9
    ISBN 0-8094-9430-2 (lib. bdg.)
    1. Indians of North America—Biography.
  2. Indians of North America—Kings and rulers.
  3. Chiefdoms—North America—Biography.
    I. Time-Life Books.
E89.M54   1993   93-22395
973'.0497'00922—dc20   CIP
[B]

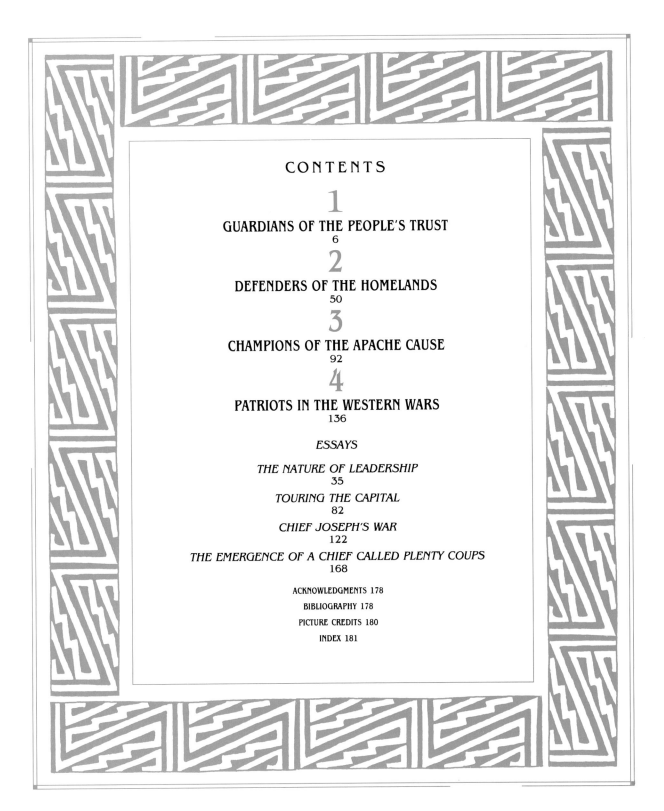

CONTENTS

1

GUARDIANS OF THE PEOPLE'S TRUST

In the years immediately following the Civil War, the Seneca Ely Samuel Parker, or Donehogawa, as his people called him, was the most acclaimed Indian in North America. A direct descendant of Jigonsaseh, the Mother of Nations, who helped the culture heroes Hiawatha and Deganawida found the historic Iroquois League, Parker held the office of Keeper of the Western Door, embodying a link to the not-so-distant past when the league's five tribes dominated the eastern woodlands. But Parker was equally celebrated in the world of the white man. A skilled civil engineer, he had fought at the siege of Vicksburg and later, as military secretary to Ulysses S. Grant, transcribed the surrender document signed by Confederate general Robert E. Lee at Appomattox. By that time, Parker had risen to the rank of brigadier general. When Grant was elected president of the United States in 1868, he made Parker commissioner of Indian affairs—the first Native American to hold that position.

Having earned the status of war chieftains for their prowess in battle, Dull Knife (far left) and Little Wolf led the Cheyenne in resistance to white encroachment during the 1860s and 1870s. The large cross worn by Dull Knife in this photograph was mainly decorative; for spiritual strength in battle, he carried the beaded lizard amulet (top left).

It was in this role of patriot and public servant that Parker was invited to the New York studio of James F. Kelley, a noted sculptor. In keeping with the contemporary custom of making busts of famous individuals, Kelley had been commissioned to do a rendering of Parker.

During their first session together, the sculptor told Parker that he considered him to be the greatest Indian who ever lived. When Parker scoffed at the notion, citing a host of other chiefs living and dead who were much "better and wiser" than himself, Kelley explained his reasoning: "I do not intend to flatter you," he said. "I mean that you are a man who has 'pierced the enemy's lines.' You have torn yourself from one environment and made yourself master of another. In this you have done more for your people than any other Indian who ever lived. You proved what an Indian of capacity could be in the white man's world. The heroes you name did not. We have no way of measuring their capacity in our standards. We do not even know exactly what they said; their speeches were all translated by interpreters. But we know what you have said as we know what you have done, and that measured by our own ideals."

"That may be true," Parker replied acidly, "but why should you test the capacity of the red man's mind in measures that may have an improper scale? Do you measure cloth with a balance or by the gallon?"

Ely Parker had put his finger precisely on the problem most whites have had in judging Indian leaders. Like James Kelley, they have perceived them in Western rather than in Indian terms. Even the word *chief* is somewhat of a misnomer, for it implies an authority that few Indian leaders possessed. The overwhelming majority of chiefs led their people by consensus, not coercion. In fact, most tribes had numerous chiefs, with different words in their language to describe each rank and jurisdiction. Parker's own Iroquois League, for example, had a ruling body of 50 *hoyarnagowar,* or "great councilors," as the Seneca called them. In addition, the Iroquois also had a lesser body of leaders, known as "solitary pine trees."

Ambrocio Martinez, elected governor of New Mexico's San Juan Pueblo in the early 1900s, holds two silver canes symbolizing his authority. One cane was given to the pueblo by the Spaniards when they ruled the Southwest; the other was presented by President Lincoln in 1863 as a gesture of amity. Still in use, such canes are passed from one pueblo leader to the next.

Such an abundance of chiefs was not uncommon among the larger Indian nations. Even the Cheyenne, whose population during the mid-19th century probably never exceeded 4,000, had 44 different chiefs: four from each of the tribe's 10 bands and four head chiefs. Collectively they formed a governing council that decided all major issues facing the community, such as the undertaking of war, the creation of alliances with a neighboring tribe, or the decision to move camp in pursuit of the buffalo herds during the communal hunting season.

The council of chiefs typically reached a decision only after engaging in lengthy public debate—and rarely went against the wishes of the majority of the people. Although the opinion of a head chief generally carried more weight than that of a lesser chief, he had no more political power and was obeyed only to the extent that his opinions made good sense. Not surprisingly, most chiefs were brilliant speakers, capable of expressing their views with clarity and eloquence in almost any setting.

In some Indian communities, sons inherited their chieftaincies from the mother's side of the family, as was the case with Ely Parker. In others, they inherited rank from their father. A few of the New England and mid-Atlantic coastal tribes had female chiefs as well. In several communities, women of childbearing age nominated candidates and passed judgment on their performance. Most frequently, a chief qualified for his position on personal merit, with a tribal council determining his worthiness.

The common proving ground was war, especially among the Plains and eastern woodlands tribes. Before a young man could join the council that advised and selected tribal leaders, he had to perform a military feat. The Crow, for example, recognized four such feats: leading a successful war party; stealing a horse from an enemy camp; being the first to touch or count coup on an enemy; and seizing an enemy's weapon in hand-to-hand combat. Once a warrior had achieved one of them, the Crow called him *batsé tse,* or "valiant man," and he was eligible to become a chief.

Although exact roles differed from tribe to tribe, a chief's main duty was to safeguard his people. Looking out for the welfare of the widows and orphans was a primary task; settling disputes between quarreling families, another. In addition to benevolence and a talent for mediation, chiefs also were noted for generosity. Among tribes of the Northwest Coast, a chief could cement his position by distributing huge quantities of trade goods and ceremonial objects to his followers. Giveaways of wealth were also common on the Plains, where a chief might spread his influence beyond his immediate band by giving away horses and food.

When it came to fighting, however, most tribes selected a different leader—a man who was chosen specifically for his skills as a warrior. A war chief was almost always someone of proven ability who had shown exceptional bravery on the battlefield as well as a sound grasp of military tactics. He was never granted authoritarian power and had to rely on his reputation to attract participants in a war party. Each successful experience in combat added to his stature. One failure, however—sometimes merely the loss of a single warrior—could tarnish his prestige and even end his career as a war chief.

Every Indian nation cherishes traditions of illustrious past leaders. With few exceptions, however, the actual lives of these ancestral chiefs remain shrouded in legends. Written history began only with the arrival of the Europeans, who chronicled the three-century-long white-Indian conflict that ended with the total military defeat of the Indian peoples. In tribe after tribe, this era of crisis called forth chiefs of heroic proportions.

Against impossible odds, some conducted unrelenting warfare; others turned their energies to seeking peace and accommodation. All of them were patriots. For the most part, however, the greatness of these men was rarely recognized until after they were dead or no longer posed a threat to American expansion. King Philip, Pontiac, Tecumseh, and contemporaries of Ely Samuel Parker such as Black Hawk, Mangas Coloradas, Victorio, Cochise, Geronimo, Quanah Parker, Red Cloud, Sitting Bull, and Crazy Horse were reviled in their time as "savages," "bandits," and "threats to civilization." But the accounts of their lives reveal qualities well worth emulation—qualities that without doubt descended through countless generations of Native Americans: loyalty, bravery, wisdom, and dedication to improving the lot of their people.

Even in the earliest days of the American colonies, a few far-sighted chiefs foresaw the trend toward dispossession. One such leader was Metacomet, the second son of Woosamequin, or Yellow Feather, the Wampanoag grand sachem known to history by his title, Massasoit. Originally, Massasoit's people ruled much of present-day Rhode Island and southern Massachusetts, including Cape Cod and the islands of Nantucket and Martha's Vineyard. But between 1616 and 1619, the years immediately preceding the Puritans' arrival at Plymouth, the Wampanoag lost half to two-thirds of their population to a plague—probably smallpox—and the 1,000 or so survivors found themselves threatened by their traditional enemies, the Narragansett, or People of the Point, who lived west of the 28-mile-long inlet off the Rhode Island coast, subsequently named Narragansett Bay after them.

Massasoit sought to improve his people's weakened position by offering the Puritans a treaty of friendship. For decades, the alliance benefited both sides. In 1636 Massasoit kept the Wampanoag out of the first major Indian-white conflict in New England, which resulted in the near destruction of the Pequot, an Algonquian-speaking tribe originally united with the Mohegan. Had Massasoit backed the Pequot, the Puritans might well have lost their foothold in the New World. The Puritans, for their part, provided the Wampanoag with ongoing protection against the Narragansett Indians, along with a steady supply of valuable trade goods. But amity exacted its price. As an increasing number of new colonists arrived from England and the coastal towns filled up, Puritan authorities demanded the right to settle on more and more of the Wampanoag land.

Chief Tlupanamabu of the Nootka Indians of the Northwest Coast wears his culture's badge of honor, a woven whaler's hat decorated, like the one at right, with images of hunters bravely harpooning whales from their small boats.

Massasoit's willingness to accommodate the English eventually led to friction between the two vastly different cultures. Many of the strict Puritans considered the Indians nothing more than agents of Satan and thus fair game for any ploy that might cause them to sign away their land. The Indians, in turn, found the English concept of property incomprehensible. A deed meant nothing to a Wampanoag, who believed in the right to hunt or grow crops on any land not in use. Some disputes went to the colonial courts, where the judges sided with their fellow whites; others ended in violence, raising tempers on both sides. After Massasoit's death in 1661, the Plymouth authorities decided to end the problem by forcing the Wampanoag into subjugation. They ordered the new grand sachem, Wamsutta—Massasoit's designated successor—to appear before them and promise loyalty.

The Mandan warrior Mató-Tópe (left) portrayed himself on the buffalo hide above as winning some of the battle victories that earned him election as tribal chief in 1837. At the top of the hide, Mató-Tópe holds off a horde of Assiniboins, represented by their retreating footprints. At the bottom, his body painted red, he uses a lance hung with feathers to defeat a Cheyenne chief.

At Massasoit's request, the Plymouth general court had given both of his sons English names. Because the court officials considered Massasoit the king of his people, they chose distinguished names from ancient history—Alexander for Wamsutta, after Alexander the Great; and Philip for Metacomet, after Philip II of Macedon, Alexander the Great's father. But an English name did not make an English subject. Wamsutta rejected the Puritan call for allegiance, prompting the authorities to send troops to haul him before them. While undergoing harsh questioning in English custody, Wamsutta fell ill. Although the English allowed the Wampanoag to carry their ailing leader back to his village on a litter, they kept his two young sons as hostages. Wamsutta died before he reached home.

The Wampanoag laid his death at the English door and turned to the new grand sachem, Metacomet, or King Philip, as the colonists would call him. Just 24 years old, King Philip already held a reputation for courage and statesmanship. He also had a clear understanding of the challenge ahead. Submission to the English, he believed, would destroy his people. The alternative was to stand and fight. He knew, however, that stemming the rising tide of white settlement would require an unprecedented cooperation among the New England tribes.

King Philip took it upon himself to create that unity. From the principal Wampanoag village of Pokanoket, located at the base of a 100-foot-high promontory called Montaup that jutted into Narragansett Bay, King Philip sent messengers to other New England tribes. The grand sachem personally journeyed to distant councils to argue for concerted action against the English. But most of the neighboring chiefs were reluctant to take on such a formidable foe.

As rumors of an Indian uprising circulated throughout the colonies, the settlers took steps to bring the Wampanoag under control. In 1671 Plymouth authorities threatened to launch a punitive expedition against Pokanoket. Not yet prepared for war, King Philip bought time by playing one Puritan colony off against another. He was able to persuade the leaders of the Massachusetts Bay Colony at Boston to intervene with Plymouth. In exchange, King Philip agreed to acknowledge Plymouth's rule by pledging an annual tribute of goods.

King Philip's intertribal alliance was still not ready when hostilities broke out four years later. The fighting was triggered by a Wampanoag traitor who divulged the grand sachem's plans to the governor of Plymouth. Events swiftly escalated. Vengeful Indians murdered the turncoat, spurring colonial authorities to hang three of King Philip's subchiefs. The

humiliating executions infuriated the Indians, and on June 20, 1675, angry warriors ransacked the town of Swansea. Three days later, an English youth shot a Wampanoag, drawing the first blood of what would become a savage, two-year conflict—what the English would call King Philip's War. The next day, the Wampanoag took revenge, killing nine whites outright and mortally wounding two others.

At first, the Indians had much the better of the fighting. From a hidden camp located in a cedar swamp to the east of Narragansett Bay, King Philip directed a series of successful raids, burning settlements and forcing the English to abandon Middleboro, a village near Plymouth. When the colonials marched on his stronghold in late July, King Philip and his followers fought them off and then slipped away, escaping to the lands of the Nipmuck in central Massachusetts.

King Philip's years of diplomacy had already borne fruit in this region. Learning of the early Wampanoag victories, the Nipmuck had attacked several colonial settlements and ambushed a party dispatched from Boston to maintain the peace. They welcomed the Wampanoag leader and

Queen Aliquippa of the Delaware Indians receives a young militia officer, George Washington, who had been sent west by Virginia's governor to scout French positions and curry favor with the Indians in 1754. Aware of the Indian custom of exchanging gifts of friendship, Washington presented the queen with a coat and a bottle of rum.

The gorget of gilded copper was presented to Iroquois leaders by the British during the French and Indian War; the silver tobacco pipe with an engraved bowl was given to Delaware chiefs in 1814 by Major General William Henry Harrison on behalf of the fledgling United States.

spread the fighting into the Connecticut River valley.

The most important addition to the alliance, however, was only partly due to King Philip's efforts. Fed up with English arrogance, many Narragansetts had long been eager to join forces with their hereditary rivals. They had already defied Plymouth by giving refuge to Alexander's widow and her Pocasset band of Wampanoags after the Puritans drove them from their homes. Worried about the Narragansett unrest, the colonists forced an unpopular treaty on the Narragansett grand sachem Canonchet. Its terms placed a price on King Philip's head and called for the capture of his followers dead or alive. But Canonchet could not ignore the sentiments of his people, and when the English leveled further demands, he refused. The settlers responded by mounting a punitive expedition. Guided by an Indian defector, colonial forces overran and burned a stockaded Narragansett village on a snowy December day. More than 600 men, women, and children perished in the raging inferno, "terribly barbecued" according to the account of Cotton Mather, the Puritan cleric. But Canonchet and more than 2,000 of his people escaped to join the Wampanoag and Nipmuck in central Massachusetts.

Augmented by his former enemies, King Philip launched a new wave of attacks in February 1676. His advice to the war parties was simple: Burn buildings and kill their inhabitants until all the whites are dead or in flight. Soon farms and villages throughout southern New England were in flames. In May the Indians daringly burned 16 homesteads within five miles of Plymouth itself. By the end of spring, his coalition had struck 52 of the 90 settlements, destroying 12 completely, heavily damaging many others, and killing more than 600 whites. King Philip's knife was near the heart of the English colonies, and victory seemed at hand.

In fact, the bold foray into Plymouth was King Philip's last great success. The Indians had no experience in sustaining a prolonged military campaign, and when their victories only increased English resistance, many began to question King Philip's leadership. The grand sachem used all of his persuasive powers to hold his forces together. A year of fighting had used up or destroyed most of the Indians' food, forcing some warriors to return to their gardens and hunting grounds in order to feed their hungry families.

By this time, the colonists had determined to eradicate the Indian nations once and for all. They sent even more troops into the field, including Indian auxiliaries from the Pequot, Mohegan, and Niantic tribes, along with a few dissident Wampanoags. Facing a foe that used Indian tactics, King Philip's warriors began falling victim to the same kinds of ambushes and surprise attacks they had used against the settlers. A combined English and Indian force captured and executed Canonchet. The Narragansett then suffered a series of disastrous setbacks. Increasingly isolated, bands of Nipmucks began surrendering. Most telling, however, was an act of treachery by a group of King Philip's own people.

By early summer of 1676, the Saconet band of the Wampanoag sued for peace. In the hope of winning good treatment, one of the Saconet war chiefs offered to lead the English to the grand sachem's camp. On July 20, a mixed company of Indians and colonial volunteers fell upon King Philip in a swamp near present-day Bridgewater, Massachusetts. The grand sachem escaped, but 173 of his people were killed or captured. His uncle and chief adviser, Unkompoin, was one of the dead; among the captives were King Philip's wife and nine-year-old son. They, along with many other Wampanoags, suffered the same cruel fate as many of the Pequots 40 years earlier: The Puritans sold them as slaves to English planters in the West Indies for a few pounds sterling each.

"My heart breaks," King Philip reportedly cried out after the battle; "now I am ready to die." With his alliance destroyed, and his own band dwindling, he made his way back to Pokanoket. The village could only be a deathtrap, but King Philip was determined to die in his ancestral home. His defiance of the English, however, still burned brightly. When a warrior suggested making peace, he ordered the man killed, triggering a final act

The marshy terrain of Cape Cod was the realm of the Wampanoag, who were led by King Philip in a bloody but ill-fated attempt to drive British colonists from the ancient homelands of the Indians in Massachusetts and Rhode Island.

of treason. The Indian's brother defected to the English, offering them the head of the Wampanoag grand sachem.

At dawn on August 12, 1676, King Philip awoke to a volley of musket fire crashing into the brush shelters of his camp. Springing to his feet, he raced for the safety of the woods. There would be no refuge this time, however. He ran directly into an ambush and fell dead with a musket ball through the heart. It is said that King Philip's head was cut off and left on display at the Plymouth settlement for 20 years. With him died the last hope of preserving the birthright of the New England Indians.

Nearly a century would pass before the Indians would mount a resistance movement to rival King Philip's. The new war took place beyond the Appalachian Mountains, far from the centers of colonial power. But the intent of its instigator, an energetic and dynamic Ottawa war chief named Pontiac, was the same—to forestall English occupation of Indian land.

The territory in question had long been claimed by the king of France. Even before the Puritans and other English colonists began settling the Atlantic seaboard, French explorers and missionaries had pushed deep into the heart of North America, establishing a string of forts and trading posts along the Saint Lawrence River and in the forests and river valleys that stretched from western Pennsylvania and New York to the Great Lakes. Many decades later, the Americans would refer to this region as the Northwest Territory. The French called it *Pays d'en haut*—the Upper Country.

The Frenchmen who maintained this empire were a hardy breed of traders, priests, and trappers. Except along the Saint Lawrence, they were few in number. Farming was of little consequence; the Upper Country's value was as a source of furs for trade with Europe. The French organized the interior tribes into a vast trading system that sent flotillas of fur-laden canoes down the Saint Lawrence to the frontier towns of Montreal and Quebec. Most Indians found it easy to accept the French *habitants,* who often took Indian wives and made few demands, desiring only furs and the land under their forts and trading posts. The guns and other manufactured goods that the French provided the Indians made accommodation all the easier.

Among the tribes the French befriended were the Ottawa, first encountered along Georgian Bay on Lake Huron's north shore (present-day Ontario) in 1615. The Ottawa lived in many separate villages, each with its own chief. They hunted, fished, and

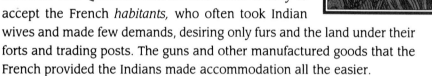

tended plots of corn, but were best known as traders (the name *Ottawa* comes from an Algonquian word meaning "to buy and sell"). Ottawa men routinely journeyed hundreds of miles, on foot or by canoe, carrying cornmeal, tobacco, furs, roots, herbs, shells, precious metals, and other valuables from tribe to tribe.

The arrival of the European fur traders changed the Indian trade network profoundly—the French along the Saint Lawrence River and Great Lakes, the British and Dutch along the Atlantic seaboard and Hudson River. Trade with the whites soon became paramount, with furs harvested in the woodlands exchanged for arms and trade goods. The insatiable European demand led to violent competition among the tribes for the steadily

Adorned in chief's regalia, King Philip appears in a detail from a map of the United States published in 1844 (top). The tobacco pipe, carved of steatite and thought to be Philip's, was unearthed from a 17th-century Indian burial ground near the chief's Rhode Island dwelling.

dwindling supply of pelts. In the 1640s, the rivalry between the French-allied Huron, or Wyandot as they called themselves, and the British-backed Iroquois exploded into a brutal war that left the Wyandot all but annihilated. Wyandot survivors either sought refuge with the French near Quebec or fled into territory that later became Michigan, Wisconsin, Ohio, and Ontario. The Ottawa, who had been selling furs to the Wyandot for resale to the French, moved into the void. But the Iroquois attacked them, too, forcing them westward as far as the Mississippi River in 1657. Strengthened by alliances with other tribes, they managed to return in the 1670s and reestablish trade links with the French, using the Ottawa River to pass well north of the Great Lakes. By the 1680s, the Ottawa provided two-thirds of the beaver pelts sold to the French. Increasingly strong and wealthy, they created a network of Indian trading partners from the Appalachian Mountains to the Mississippi.

Like every tribe that traded with whites, the Ottawa experienced great cultural changes. After a century of contact, they still had not accepted the Roman Catholicism of the Jesuit Black Robes, but the European influence on their society was pervasive. Steel and iron hatchets and knives had supplanted stone tools; brass kettles had replaced clay pots and tightly woven baskets for cooking; clothes were made of wool and cotton fabrics instead of animal skins; and most important, warriors came to rely almost entirely on guns for hunting and fighting.

Pontiac was born into this decidedly mixed culture in 1720, on the Maumee River in present-day Ohio. His father is thought to have been an Ottawa subchief and his mother an Ojibwa from the Lake Superior region. Tall and powerfully built, Pontiac began winning honors in intertribal conflicts while still a teenager, and before long, he was taking part in French-sponsored raids against the English.

The frontier conflict between the two European powers had been simmering for decades when, in the 1740s, British traders began crossing the Alleghenies to challenge the French grip on the Upper Country fur trade. By offering the Indians superior trade goods for fewer pelts, the British caused some tribes to switch allegiance. But the Ottawa stuck by their traditional benefactors. When the British-French rivalry burst into full-scale war in the 1750s, the Ottawa and most of the other western tribes sided with France and shared the glory and spoils of numerous victories, including the rout of Major General Edward Braddock's army in western Pennsylvania in 1755. The war's outcome, however, was determined not by these frontier clashes, but by European-style battles fought before the distant French fortresses of Canada. Compelled by defeats at Louisburg and Quebec, the French relinquished their Canadian holdings in 1760.

The French surrender stunned the Indians, although its full consequences took time to unfold. Pontiac was present in November 1760, when British troops disembarked from a fleet of whaleboats to claim Fort Detroit, on the site of the present-day city. During conferences with leaders of the surrounding Ottawa, Wyandot, and Potawatomi villages, George Croghan, the British Indian agent, assured the Indians that their new white neighbors intended to continue French policies. Croghan's diplomatic explanations left out one essential point, however: British claim to ownership of the entire region. To Sir Jeffrey Amherst, the British commander in chief in North America, this meant that all residents of the territory, Indian or white, were now subjects of the English Crown.

Amherst, who had previously won fame fighting in Europe in the War of the Austrian Succession, was contemptuous of all Indians. "The only true method of treating the savages," he once said, "is to keep them in proper subjection and punish, without exception, the transgressors." To Amherst, a transgression meant any failure to obey his dictates. Thus, he bridled when his head Indian agent, Sir William Johnson, recommended supplying the Indians at Detroit with arms, ammunition, and

The Ojibwa chief Okeemakeequid wears a deerskin cape and feathered headdress given him by a Sioux leader after the two warring tribes declared peace in 1825. At right are the chief's war club and a fur stole, also presented to Okeemakeequid by the Sioux during the ritual exchange of gifts that traditionally accompanied peace parleys.

clothing as the French had done. Having lived among the Iroquois, and fathered several children by a Mohawk woman, Johnson understood the importance the Indians placed on gift giving. But the suggestion only outraged Amherst. "When men of whatsoever race behave ill, they must be punished not bribed," Amherst replied. The British general then ordered his commanders to stop distributing goods to Indian visitors and prohibited all transactions other than those conducted at authorized trading posts.

The new policy confused and angered the Native Americans. The denial of ammunition and emergency food rations caused distress in some villages; hunters resented the need for long, inconvenient trips to the trading posts to sell their pelts; and those Indians with a taste for rum were not pleased when their supply was cut off. During this unsettled time, Pontiac began to speak out against the British.

Pontiac's military exploits during the French and Indian War had already won him widespread recognition. Now, however, he rose to leadership on the basis of another skill—his oratory. Pontiac was capable of holding an audience rapt for hours. Whites who met him came away impressed. One observer described him as "proud, vindictive, warlike, and easily offended." Another found him "commanding and imperious." Like most Ottawa warriors, Pontiac was probably heavily tattooed, and wore his hair short and upright in front. He usually decorated himself with ear beads, a stone in his nose, and silver bracelets.

As this formidable man began to sway tribal councils against the British, George Croghan and Sir William Johnson sought a means of defusing the situation. In the late summer of 1761, they convened a conference at Detroit. The Ottawa chose a chief named Macatepilesis to speak for them at the meeting. After Macatepilesis had delivered a mild address, Croghan and Johnson thanked the Indians for their friendship, but offered them nothing in return. The British agents dared not reveal Amherst's policies, but neither could they promise redress for the Indians' grievances. At the conclusion of the gathering, Pontiac boldly stood up and voiced the growing Indian resentment. No longer constrained by French competition, British traders, he declared, were charging high prices for shoddy goods and often cheating the Indians outright.

France and Britain were not yet at peace, and despite the cession of Canada, France still claimed Louisiana and the territory along the Mississippi River. In early 1762, a rumor spread that the French and the Spaniards were preparing a joint expedition that would ascend the Mississippi from New Orleans and retake Canada. Pontiac made the most of the turmoil to enlist new supporters. He spoke to ever-larger audiences, who in turn spread his warlike message from village to village. During the summer of 1762, he convened a secret meeting of the Ottawa, Ojibwa, Wyandot, and Potawatomi and later conveyed word to the Shawnee and Delaware peoples of the Ohio River valley. Tension continued to build during the following winter, aggravated by reports of British settlers moving into Shawnee and Delaware lands. This new threat gave rise to a religious movement among the Delaware that Pontiac was quick to exploit.

A Delaware holy man by the name of Neolin had begun preaching that the decline in Indian fortunes had two root causes: the corrupting influence of the whites and the Indians' own sinfulness. Improper behavior, especially addiction to the white man's rum and the failure to observe proper rituals, had angered the manitous, or Indian guardian spirits. In order to restore prosperity, Neolin prescribed temperance, monogamy, self-sufficiency, and intertribal peace.

Pontiac modified Neolin's message to render it anti-British rather than antiwhite. His call for war and the prophecy spread like wildfire through a region already kindled by the circulation of Seneca war belts—lengths of wampum indicating that the powerful westernmost member of the Iroquois League intended to fight its former ally, the British. Pontiac received a number of pledges to join him in his endeavor, and French traders offered him assurances that help would be forthcoming from Louisiana. The time had come to lay plans for a concerted attack.

In April of 1763, Pontiac revealed his thinking to a secret council of 400 Ottawa, Wyandot, and Potawatomi warriors and chiefs. He spoke to the gathering about the incessant British wrongdoing and of the great victories that had been won over them in years past. He reminded his

Chief Pontiac of the Ottawa organized a violent rebellion against British rule, persuading warriors from no fewer than 10 tribes to attack 13 English forts in the spring of 1763. The Indians captured all but four of the British bastions.

audience of the message Neolin had received from Gitche Manitou, the Master of Life: "The land on which you live I have made for you, and not for others. Why do you suffer the white men to dwell among you?" "As for these English," Pontiac continued to quote, "these dogs dressed in red, who have come to rob you of your hunting grounds, and drive away the game—you must lift the hatchet against them. Wipe them from the face of the earth, and then you will win my favor back again, and once more be happy and prosperous. The children of your great father, the king of France, are not like the English. Never forget that they are your brethren. They are very dear to me, for they love the red men, and understand the true mode of worshiping me."

Pontiac proposed an attack on Fort Detroit and laid out his plan before the assembly. The warriors would return to their villages to prepare for the coming battle, he said, while he scouted the fort's defenses. The results would be discussed at another council where final plans would be made. As his followers prepared for war, Pontiac dispatched runners carrying war belts to other tribes, urging them to join the revolt.

Gaining entry to the fort was not difficult. On May 1, Pontiac and approximately 50 warriors offered to entertain the British officers who were stationed there with a ceremonial dance. While the majority of the Indians engaged in a lively performance, others drifted off to check on the locations of guns, buildings, and guard posts. At day's end, Pontiac took his leave, assuring Major Henry Gladwin, the commander of the fort, that he would return in a few days for a council of goodwill—a council, he later explained to his followers, that would end with the deaths of all the British. Pontiac and his warriors planned to enter the fort, followed by the men and women from his village, each one bearing a concealed weapon. At his signal, the Ottawas would overpower their unsuspecting hosts, while the Wyandots and Potawatomis attacked any whites who happened to be outside the fort.

PONTIAC IN COUNCIL.

Early on May 7, Pontiac led 300 Indians across the Detroit River and approached the fort. Wrapped in blankets that concealed knives, hatchets, and sawed-off muskets, they pushed through the east gate. Pontiac, in the lead, carried a wampum belt. If he presented the belt to the post commander with its green side showing, the attack was to begin at once. But a glance around the fort was enough to show Pontiac that his plan could not work. All the post buildings were locked, the sentries were at double strength, and the remainder of the 120-member garrison was assembled on the parade ground. The Indians watched for a flash of green as the chief approached Major Gladwin. But Pontiac, fearing disaster, changed his plans on the spot. He angrily condemned Gladwin for this unfriendly greeting, suggesting that "some bad bird had given you ill news of us." After accepting a few token gifts, Pontiac led his followers away.

Gladwin had in fact been forewarned—either by an Indian ally or by a disaffected French trader who might have witnessed the war dances in the villages, or seen the Indians cutting down their musket barrels. Whatever the source of the betrayal, Pontiac found himself on uncertain ground with his own warriors, who criticized him for not giving the signal to attack. He promised them another opportunity, and two days later, he attempted to bluster his way back into the fort. But this time, Gladwin would agree to admit the Indians only in small groups, and the furious Pontiac had to return to his village empty-handed. There he announced that the war would begin immediately. Having failed to take the fort by stealth, he would now besiege it, killing all the Englishmen found outside the walls and starving those within. In the meantime, raiding parties would fan out to attack other British forts while runners carried war belts to enlist the help of the neighboring tribes.

The fighting began auspiciously. On the first day, Pontiac's warriors killed nine people around Fort Detroit and took several prisoners. A band of Ojibwas wiped out a surveying party on nearby Lake Saint Clair. Wyandots guarding the Detroit River intercepted five boats carrying supplies and trade goods from Niagara, a British fort and depot located at the east-

Holding up a symbolic war belt made of wampum, Pontiac (inset) exhorts other chiefs to join him in the fight against arrogant British rule. In the 19th-century engraving shown below, he stands amid more than 400 warriors of the Ottawa, Wyandot, and Potawatomi tribes at the famous council he called in April 1763, at which he used his great power as an orator to persuade them to cooperate in his rebellion.

ern end of Lake Erie. One week afterward, a band of Ottawas and Wyandots captured Fort Sandusky, 60 miles to the east on the south shore of Lake Erie. By the end of May, a band of Potawatomis had taken Fort Saint Joseph, 160 miles to the west, near today's South Bend, Indiana, while another Potawatomi war party had seized Fort Miami, on the Maumee River, 140 miles to the southwest.

Runners soon reached Pontiac with even better news. Tribes to the east and west, responding to his call, had risen against the British in their own territories, seizing forts and wiping out settlements. The Delaware laid siege to Fort Pitt (on the site of present-day Pittsburgh), and the Ojibwa slaughtered or captured the entire garrison at Fort Michilimackinac on the strategic strait between Lakes Huron and Michigan. Pontiac's own warriors surprised a British supply fleet that was docked at Point Pelee, an overnight encampment 30 miles southeast of Detroit; less than half of the fleet's 96-man troop detachment escaped the attack. The triumphant Indians then sailed eight huge supply canoes filled with provisions and prisoners past the fort to their own villages.

By the end of June, less than two months after the first shots were fired at Detroit, Pontiac and his allies had attacked 13 British forts and captured nine. And two of the remaining four, Fort Pitt and Fort Detroit, were under siege. In all, the Indians probably inflicted more than 2,000

Their weapons concealed by their blankets, warriors led by Pontiac (standing, with wampum) meet with a suspicious Major Henry Gladwin during their abortive attempt to seize Fort Detroit while pretending to be on a peacemaking mission.

Indian warriors under the command of Pontiac launch an attack against Fort Detroit in one of several thwarted attempts to take the stockade by storm. Pontiac's failure to capture the fort after a six-month siege helped doom his rebellion.

casualties. Many of the surviving British troops and settlers fled to safety east of the Appalachians.

At this high point in their struggle, however, the Indians received disconcerting reports of the signing of a peace treaty between France and Britain, officially concluding their North American conflict. Pontiac gave little credence to the bad news, persisting in his belief that the king of France would send troops to support him. But a number of his allies had begun to question the wisdom of continued warfare. The British, moreover, were not about to yield to what Sir Jeffrey Amherst called "such a wretched enemy as the Indians."

Outraged by the news of disaster on the frontier, Amherst directed

Captain James Dalyell to assemble detachments to relieve the forces at Detroit. Embarking from Niagara with 260 men, Dalyell took advantage of a heavy fog to sneak past the Indians on the Detroit River, arriving at the fort on July 28. He planned to give his men two days of rest, then march under cover of darkness for a surprise attack on Pontiac's main camp, situated several miles upriver.

Anticipating Dalyell's movement, Pontiac set up an ambush at a narrow bridge two miles from the fort. Shortly before dawn he sprang the trap on the unsuspecting British, who were silhouetted by a bright moon. The Indians fired on the troops from concealed positions on both sides of the column, then closed in. They kept the British surrounded for more than an hour, blocking their retreat with heavy fire from a fortified flanking position. Finally, the wounded Dalyell led a desperate assault that cleared the road, although he was shot dead in the charge. His detachment staggered back to Detroit to count its casualties: 20 dead, 34 wounded, and several lost as prisoners.

The British gave a new name, Bloody Run, to the stream where Pontiac won his victory, but their determination was unshaken. The survivors of Dalyell's force more than doubled the garrison at Detroit, and Gladwin soon began using this new strength to mount small raids against the Indians. News of Bloody Run so angered Amherst that he proposed spreading smallpox among the Indians by offering them germ-laden blankets. He ordered the commander of a column bound for Detroit to treat the Indians "not as a generous enemy, but as the vilest race of beings that ever infested the earth, and whose riddance from it must be esteemed a meritorious act." As to Pontiac, Amherst offered a reward of £100 to the man who killed him, and soon doubled the offer.

Fort Detroit proved a tough nut to crack for Pontiac and his 870 warriors. Despite their efforts, British supplies and reinforcements continued to trickle through the siege lines, and by September, the fort was stronger than ever. Some of Pontiac's followers began to lose patience. In addition, other Indians were outraged by the ritual torture and cannibalism of British prisoners, acts they considered counter to the moral teachings of Neolin. The son of one Ojibwa chief came all the way from upper Michigan to deliver his father's rebuke to Pontiac.

Pontiac badly needed a battlefield victory. In the early autumn, he dispatched a fleet of canoes against a British supply schooner. The attack ended in disaster. The schooner's guns cut the raiding force to pieces, and as the Indians withdrew with many dead and wounded, the ship pro-

Executing a spectacular ruse, Ojibwa and Sauk warriors stage a game of lacrosse outside Fort Michilimackinac as the British garrison looks on. When an Ojibwa shot a ball into the fort, the British opened the gate so it could be retrieved, and the warriors flooded in, seizing the stronghold and capturing 70 defenders.

ceeded to Fort Detroit with its cargo. Small groups of warriors had already broken away; now larger numbers began to defect. The upheaval at Detroit mirrored dissension throughout the region. Although hatred of the British remained widespread, many Indians were tired of the killing and longed to resume trade relations with the British.

By October the remaining warriors began drifting off to their hunting grounds to lay in a supply of meat for winter. An impassioned plea from Pontiac kept a nucleus of fighters for a few more days, but no powers of persuasion could overcome the effect of a letter he received late in the month, from Captain Louis St. Ange de Bellerive, the commandant of Fort de Chartres, a French outpost on the Mississippi. The kings of England and France had indeed made peace, the letter said, and the commandant begged Pontiac to do the same. The French and the English were now brothers, St. Ange wrote; attacking one would make enemies of both.

The shattering impact of this information was evident in the letter that Pontiac dictated and dispatched to Gladwin the following day. "My Brother," it read, "the word that my father has sent me to make peace I have accepted; all my young men have buried their hatchets. I think you

THE OJIBWA'S IRISH CHIEF

One Ojibwa chief in good standing during the Revolutionary period was not an Indian at all but an Irish baronet by the name of Sir John Caldwell. A British officer stationed at Forts Niagara and Detroit from 1774 to 1780, Caldwell paid official visits to Indian villages, particularly the Ojibwa, to maintain the alliances between the Indians and the Crown against the American colonists. In the process, the Irishman developed respect and enthusiasm for the Indian way of life and amassed a treasure-trove of Native American artifacts. The Ojibwa returned the admiration by electing Caldwell a chief of the tribe and giving him an Indian name, Apatto, or Runner.

Choice items from Caldwell's collection at right—all displayed in the portrait below—include a tomahawk and a decorated skin knife sheath. The silver ear pendants, gorgets, and iron knife were trade goods that were made for barter with the Indians by Canadian, British, and American artisans.

Back in Ireland after the Revolution, Caldwell commissioned a portrait of himself wearing some of the Indian finery he had collected, notably the headdress, which he embellished with ostrich feathers; a nose piece; moccasins with deer-hair fringing; and red cloth leggings held up with garters of white beads. In his hand is a purple wampum belt.

will forget the bad things that have taken place for some time past. Like-
wise I shall forget what you may have done to me, in order to think of
nothing but good. I, the Ojibwa, the Huron, we are ready to speak with
you when you ask us. Give us an answer. I am sending this resolution in
order that you may see it. If you are as kind as I, you will make me a reply.
I wish you a good day. Pontiac."

Gladwin replied that he must await instructions from Sir Jeffrey Amherst. Those instructions never came, for Amherst had been relieved in
early October. His replacement, the more conciliatory Major General Thomas Gage, believed that fighting the western Indians was useless, and directed his subordinates to seek peace. It would be a lengthy process,
however. By mid-November, no orders had reached Gladwin. Tired of
waiting for an audience, Pontiac left Detroit with a group of loyal Ottawas
to set up a winter camp along the Maumee River.

Pontiac nursed his bitterness through the months of cold weather,
and when spring arrived, he traveled among the tribes of the Illinois
country. He spoke of the warfare that continued to rage on the Pennsylvania and Ohio frontier, urging his listeners to join the fight. His deputies
traveled far down the Mississippi River in an effort to win the support of
the southern tribes. Their mission ended in failure, however, and by the
late summer of 1764, the Seneca, Menominee, Sauk, and Fox had all
signed treaties with the British. Virtually every village in the region was
rent by factionalism; even many of Pontiac's own Ottawas leaned toward
accommodation with the new white power.

In September, Pontiac decided to explore the possibility of coexistence with the British. He sent a peace belt to the new commander at Detroit, Colonel John Bradstreet, who had recently arrived at the fort with an
army of 1,200 men—huge by frontier standards—and a mandate to pacify
the territory either by treaty or by force. Convinced that Pontiac was irrep-
arably weakened, Bradstreet chopped the peace belt to pieces. The Indians, whose tradition required at least a show of respect in negotiations,
were outraged by his action, and Pontiac concluded that he would gain
nothing by dealing with the British.

Bradstreet's estimate of Pontiac proved disastrously wrong. The Ottawa war chief had matured into an adroit politician, and he now returned
to the arduous work of alliance building. His followers among the Ojibwa
and Miami expressed a willingness to fight if war flared up again. The
Illinois tribes who occupied a region the French had ceded to Britain
promised they would resist any British incursions. Many of the French

settlers also backed Pontiac, supplying his allies with powder and shot in the hope of blocking British expansion.

By the spring of 1765, Pontiac had restored his prestige to the point that the British decided he was the key to a lasting peace. Events had also forced another change in his outlook. The Shawnee and Delaware had made peace with the British. Now the French commandant at Fort de Chartres, Captain St. Ange, began to sway Pontiac with appeals for a peaceful transfer of power to the British. St. Ange persuaded him to talk with the newly arrived Lieutenant Alexander Fraser, dispatched by General Gage to befriend the western tribes.

Fraser, a better diplomat than Bradstreet, offered Pontiac a peace belt and assured the chief that the British considered him a brother, as a result of a treaty negotiated by Bradstreet with a faction of the Ottawa Nation the previous fall. Summoning Pontiac and his Illinois allies to council on April 18, Fraser and St. Ange made clear the French-British resolve to end hostilities. This joint announcement proved decisive. Rising slowly to face St. Ange, Pontiac solemnly declared that his war was over.

Peacemaking, however, would prove an arduous test for Pontiac's statesmanship. He agreed to meet with George Croghan, the Indian agent. In early May, Fraser, Pontiac, and the Illinois chiefs waited for Croghan in Ouiatenon, a French town on the Wabash near present-day Lafayette, Indiana. After several days of sitting, the Illinois, incensed by Croghan's failure to appear, abruptly abandoned the peace plan. Sensing danger, Pontiac warned Fraser to flee immediately.

Pontiac's new role as peacemaker was now threatened by the same forces he had exploited as a war leader. Young warriors among the Illinois, never bested in combat by the British, were reluctant to yield any territory. Some of the French settlers supported their resistance, and spread rumors of attacks against Illinois villages by British forces and their Cherokee allies. In late May, an Illinois war party attacked George Croghan's party, which had finally reached the region. Although Croghan survived, many of his escort were killed, including three Shawnee chiefs.

The attack changed Pontiac's fortunes again. The death of the Shawnees meant near-certain retaliation by that tribe and its allies, all supported by the British. Faced with a war they could not win, the elders of the Illinois villages repudiated the actions of their warriors and sought peace. Pontiac, who was still lingering among the Illinois after the debacle at

Ouiatenon, now emerged as the most credible mediator. The British welcomed him in this new role, and in the summer of 1765, Pontiac made his final peace in a conference at Detroit.

The agreement ended Pontiac's career as an alliance chieftain. The coming of peace removed incentives for regional action, and leadership of the individual tribes devolved to the traditional village, clan, and band units. The British, however, continued to treat Pontiac as if he were leader of all the region's tribes. Perhaps flattered by the recognition, Pontiac began to play the part. At a British-sponsored council of chiefs convened at Niagara in 1766, he claimed to speak "in the name of all the nations to the westward whom I command."

The pronouncement served only to further diminish his reputation, which was already tarnished by the attention he had received from the British. Returning from the conference, he found little support, even among his own Ottawas. The younger warriors showed him no respect and refused to accept him as a leader. Humiliated, Pontiac left his village in 1768 to live with relatives in the Illinois country.

He found no warmer welcome there. Two years earlier, he had stabbed an Illinois chief in a quarrel, and they received him with fear and resentment. When Pontiac departed to hunt during the winter, a rumor spread that he intended to return in the spring with 150 canoe loads of Ottawa warriors. He did in fact return, but only with two sons and a handful of supporters. On April 20, 1769, he entered a trading store in the French village of Cahokia, on the Mississippi, with an apparently friendly member of the Peoria band of the Illinois. The two men had just left the store when the warrior struck Pontiac from behind with a club, then stabbed him. The Ottawa war chief died where he fell. The one-time leader of thousands had not a single follower to avenge his death.

THE NATURE OF LEADERSHIP

The strength of a chief lay in his knowledge of his people and their traditions. "Boys were trained so that should the honor of being made chief come to them, they would be ready," explained Luther Standing Bear, a Lakota Sioux. "In their minds were stored the history and lore of their tribe, the events of migration and travel, the tales and prophecies of wise men, battles and victories, and secrets the brotherhood of animals shared with the medicine men." Steeped in such collective wisdom, a man who attained leadership felt obligated to his followers. Above all, Luther Standing Bear declared, a chief "must be a giver and not a receiver—a man of self-denial."

To be sure, the leaders of various tribes exhibited that essential trait of generosity in markedly different ways. The Algonquian-speaking peoples of the mid-Atlantic region, the southeastern tribes, and the Pacific Northwest Indians concentrated considerable power and wealth in the hands of their chiefs, who then redistributed the bounty to subordinates—or dedicated it to the spirits—in rituals that ennobled the leader and inspired his community.

Across the western interior, by contrast, seminomadic tribes generally affirmed their independence by limiting the power of their numerous chiefs and denying them any tribute other than that of respect. Seldom did one man have authority to speak for the entire tribe. Federal officials struggling to negotiate a treaty with a tribe often singled out a leader—or a man who appeared sympathetic to the government—and dubbed him "chief" of his entire nation. If that tribe subsequently violated an agreement, the officials were quick to accuse the new spokesman of duplicity, failing to realize that his authority was far from absolute and that even those who recognized him as chief were free to disobey or disclaim him.

In such circumstances, self-denial was indeed a prerequisite for leadership, for the chief not only had to work tirelessly for the good of his people but also had to be ready to relinquish his command at any time. Nonetheless, the distinction of being looked to for support by the tribe was a great reward in itself. And the chief's sense of pride was reinforced by the splendid emblems of honor he was entitled to wear or carry. Pictured on the following pages, these tokens of leadership tell of a power that transcended the individual chief and embodied the eternal dreams of his people.

A Sioux leader puffs a sacred pipe in this early drawing by a Jesuit. The misnomer "roi" (king) was often applied to eminent Indians.

This majestic eagle-feather war bonnet was worn by an Arapaho chief, Yellow Calf, to signal that he had successfully performed the courageous feats expected of a leader.

IN COMMAND ON THE GREAT PLAINS

In the culture of the far-ranging Plains Indians, military prowess was considered an essential criterion for leadership. Although any warrior could aspire to the status of chief, he first was required to perform certain brave deeds, or coups, including the feat of touching a live enemy in battle.

Among the Arapaho and some other tribes, a warrior might celebrate the accomplishment of a coup by depicting the event on the outside of his tipi or by adding a feather to his bonnet—as a consequence, feathered bonnets be-

came emblems of chieftaincy. Feathers held no special meaning for the Comanche Indians, however. In contrast, their leading warriors frequently adorned themselves with the scalp and horns of a buffalo.

Military skills alone were not sufficient to achieve the status of chief, however. A true leader also had to forge a link with the spirit world by means of a dream or vision. The beings, events, or scenes beheld during such revelations were subsequently depicted on various objects belonging to the chief, including war shields, in order to gain supernatural protection.

At public celebrations, a war chief recited his battle exploits by striking a post with a stick like the one at left. As he recounted each coup, he landed another blow.

Before a raid, leading Comanche warriors wore buffalo headdresses such as this as a symbol of their fighting ability.

Atsina chief and medicine man Niä-tóhosä performs his role as a spiritual leader by smoking a sacred pipe in this 1833 watercolor by Karl Bodmer.

Horses and warriors decorate the tipi of Sioux chief Old Bull (foreground) at a camp in North Dakota about 1900. The drawings depict feats attributed to the chief at the Battle of the Little Bighorn in 1876.

Chief Dohausen of the Kiowa Indians exudes stolid confidence in this portrait by George Catlin. He was the tribe's principal leader from 1833 to 1866. When he died, his nephew inherited his shield (opposite).

Visiting Washington, D.C., in 1916, Bird Rattler (far right) sits for a photograph with federal officials and two fellow chiefs. He is wearing a traditional, straight-up Blackfeet headdress with ermine tails, which denote leadership.

Prompted by a vi-
sion, this painted
shield was inherited
by Chief Dohausen
from his father or
grandfather. Blue
triangles at the rim
represent the sacred
mountains of the
Kiowa; the center
circle signifies the
Kiowa camp circle.

Photographed in 1923 by Edward Curtis, a Hupa elder displays his rare albino deerskin, used in the sacred White Deerskin Dance.

Obsidian blades such as the one at right, measuring eight and one half inches in length, were preserved by leading families and used during deerskin dances.

Wearing woodpecker-scalp headdresses, Hupas prepare for the Jump Dance. Leaders prided themselves on their ability to "put up a whole dance," or outfit a troupe of 12 or more dancers.

A Hupa man gauges the value of a string of dentalium shells against a measure tattooed on his forearm. Obtained from waters off Vancouver Island, the coveted shells were a form of currency.

These strings of slender dentalium shells and a six-inch-long elk-horn purse were among the possessions of an 18th-century Yurok Indian.

CALIFORNIA'S MAGNANIMOUS MEN OF WEALTH

Among the Hupa, Yurok, and Karok peoples who lived along the lush banks of the Klamath River in northwestern California, chiefs used their acquired treasures in ceremonies designed to ensure that Nature would continue to offer up its gifts. The surrounding generous environment made food readily available: The redwood forests provided abundant supplies of acorns, berries, and game; and the Klamath and its tributaries teemed with salmon and other spawning fish.

With such bounty close at hand, Indians had time to pursue or obtain through trade sacred objects that allowed them to perform thanksgiving ceremonies. These objects included the skins of rare albino deer and the red-feathered scalps of pileated woodpeckers, which were fashioned into headdresses. Those treasures usually belonged to privileged families, whose leaders in turn enriched the community by staging rituals such as the Jump Dance, at which men wearing the scarlet headdresses shown at left spiritually replenished the waters with salmon. As the Karok express it, such ceremonies serve to "renew the world." If a chief squandered his sacred trust and failed to pass along his treasures to the next generation, his heir became a commoner, and leadership passed to a more prosperous man who was able to sponsor the vital ceremonies.

RULING CLANS OF THE WOODLANDS

In the woodlands of the Northeast and the Great Lakes region, leadership positions were sometimes restricted to men who belonged to certain clans: societies whose members considered themselves relatives of a common spiritual ancestor, usually an animal or mythical being. The selected chief drew on the power of that being and invoked its help and protection.

The Menominee, for example, chose their principal chief from the clan dedicated to the Great Ancestral Bear, a beast revered by many tribes for its strength. When war broke out, the tribe sought temporary leadership from the Thunder Clan, whose members were not only fierce fighters but also keepers of the tribe's war bundles. The bundles contained amulets invested with a spiritual power. The Mesquakie, or Fox, Indians turned to their own Bear Clan to fill the role of peacetime chief. A war chief, on the other hand, traditionally a member of the Fox Clan, could by the early 19th century be a capable fighter from any clan.

According to custom, such leaders wore objects that invoked the spiritual power of their clan guardian. But during the 17th and 18th centuries, some leaders came to favor decorative items made from glass beads or other trade goods that reflected wealth and alliances with other peoples.

Its handle fashioned from an eagle's head and its vanes made from eagle feathers, this ceremonial Fox fan was used by chiefs or other prominent men. Like many Indians, the Fox revered the eagle.

In this 1837 portrait, Chief Nesouaquoit of the Fox wears an animalskin vest symbolizing the Bear Clan, from which the Fox chose such leaders.

Made from grizzly bear claws and otter fur, necklaces like the one shown below were worn on special occasions by chiefs of the Fox and other tribes.

Beaded bandoleer bags like the one above became signs of status among the Ojibwa and other woodlands peoples. Supposedly modeled after bullet pouches, these bags were strictly decorative.

Wearing a bear-claw necklace, Moses Keokuk (center)—son of Chief Keokuk, Black Hawk's principal rival—visits Washington, D.C., in 1867.

GIFT GIVERS OF THE NORTHWEST

Like the Indians who inhabited northern California, coastal tribes from Oregon to southern Alaska were led by wealthy ruling families. Not only did these dynasties stockpile blankets, baskets, skins, dried fish, and shells, they owned territory as well, reserving for themselves stands of cedar, hunting grounds, salmon streams, and berry patches. In addition to the freedom to accumulate material possessions, a chief and his relatives claimed the exclusive right to perform special dances and rites, and to display certain crests—symbols of ancestors or mythical beings that were believed to have helped the family in the past.

Here as in California, however, leaders were expected to use their rights and privileges in a manner that benefited others. The rituals that they staged kept the community in touch with the spirits and with their blessings. And periodically, a chief, like other prominent people living in the village, redistributed his wealth by hosting an extravagant feast, known as a potlatch, at which he gave away food and gifts to the guests.

Upon the death of a coastal tribe leader, a wake is customarily held. The deceased is dressed in his regalia, and his hereditary treasures are displayed around him. Following a month of mourning, gifts are distributed to the guests in order to show that the heir, like his predecessor, is a good provider, worthy of the privileges that have been bestowed on him.

In 1878 the deceased Tlingit chief Shakes lies surrounded by his treasured belongings. He wears a grizzly-bear frontlet around his forehead, and to his right are a staff and a killer-whale hat—shown in profile opposite.

Raven, man, and frog combine to form this rattle, used by Northwest chiefs during ceremonial dances. The figures depict the transfer of supernatural power.

Topped by a killer whale—another crest of the Shakes family—the staff shown at right was carried by Chief Shakes as a sign of his eminence.

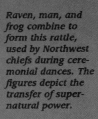

This grizzly-bear frontlet is similar to the one worn by Chief Shakes at his wake. Tlingit chiefs donned this sort of headgear to signal their exalted rank.

Worn by Chief Shakes on special occasions, a wooden hat bears the killer-whale emblem of his family. The woven rings at the top of the hat are emblems of prestige.

Stacks of blankets accumulated as gifts for a potlatch by a Tlingit chief nearly touch the ceiling of a ceremonial hall (above). As potlatch guests arrived, they were announced by the chief's herald, who sometimes stood behind a hollow post such as the one at left. The topmost carving represents the chief's mind; by speaking through its open mouth, the herald spoke for the chief.

Wearing ceremonial garb, Willie Seaweed, a Kwakiutl chief and artist, stands proudly with two coppers that are decorated with emblematic designs.

Decorated copper shields such as this one are family treasures in the Northwest. Known as coppers, they were sometimes broken up and given away at potlatches; the one here has been restored to its original condition.

HOLY MEN OF THE DESERT

In the Southwest, particularly among the Pueblo peoples, the role of chief was frequently filled by prominent members of religious societies, whose obligation it was to beseech the good-will of an array of gods that governed everything from weather and war to hunting and health.

Among the Hopi and Zuni Indians, for example, only men from certain respected families were permitted to become priests. After paying a fee made up of skins and food, a new member spent years learning the group's elaborate songs, dances, and rituals. Some of the groups, notably the Zuni Society of the Bow Priests, began as warrior societies. The Bow Priests included vestiges of their previous function, such as bows and arrows, among their emblems. This secretive religious society had a dozen grades, each with its own distinctive symbol. When Spanish colonists made contact with the Zuni, they recognized the Bow Priests as leaders of the community.

In 1882 members of the Zuni Society of the Bow Priests sit for a photograph during a visit east.

Fashioned from perforated buckskin and decorated with feathers, this cap symbolizes one of the grades of the Zuni Bow Priesthood.

Carved to resemble a lightning bolt, sticks like the one at right were planted at holy places by Zuni priests in the hope that the rain spirits would bring abundant moisture.

As shown in this late-19th-century photograph, a Hopi snake priest wears the feather head-dress of his sect, whose sacred rites summoned rain.

Wearing an elaborate mask, a Navajo shaman's assistant impersonates a god to invoke the spirit's healing power.

2

DEFENDERS OF THE HOMELANDS

Painted by an unknown artist, this resolute Indian in European dress is thought to be Tecumseh, the great Shawnee chief who fought to preserve the sovereignty of his people. Descriptions of his physical appearance are scarce, but a U.S. Army captain at Fort Knox called the epic warrior "one of the finest-looking men I ever saw."

Tecumseh, the white people called him. To his own people, he was known as Tecumtha. It was a name filled with spiritual power, an abbreviation of a phrase meaning "celestial panther lying in wait." The Shawnee chief was indeed very like a panther in war; waiting, however, was not to his taste—especially waiting for friendship to bloom between the Indians and the Long Knives, as the Shawnee called the white settlers who were pouring across the Appalachian Mountains into the Old Northwest in the early years of the 19th century. This vast wilderness, lying between the Ohio River and the Great Lakes, was the rightful domain of the Shawnee and numerous other tribes. Even the new United States government, which had recently received sovereignty over the territory from Great Britain, acknowledged the Indians' ownership—at least in theory.

"The Indians, being the prior occupants, possess the right of soil," Secretary of War Henry Knox had reasoned in a 1789 letter to President George Washington concerning the establishment of a national policy toward the continent's native inhabitants. "It cannot be taken from them unless by their free consent, or by right of conquest in case of a just war."

Congress subsequently turned Knox's ideas into laws aimed at establishing the government's relations with the Indians. The legislators determined that the various tribes were "distinct, independent, political communities" that should be treated as foreign nations. But such lofty doctrine proved to be a sham from the start. Tecumseh and other Indian leaders painfully discovered that American law, no matter how high-minded, offered them no more protection from exploitation than had the previous agreements they had signed with the British and the French. Almost without pause, whites continued to wrest the land from them—by chicanery, bribery, or simple theft.

In mid-August of 1810, Tecumseh decided to confront the man he recognized as the prime offender, William Henry Harrison, the politically ambitious governor of the Indiana Territory, who three decades later would parlay his record as an Indian fighter into the presidency of the United States. Harrison had recently extracted three million acres from a few pliant chiefs in return for a paltry assortment of trade goods and a small annuity. He shared none of Henry Knox's enlightenment toward the Indians, at least not in regard to those still living in the former Northwest Territory. "Is one of the fairest portions of the globe to remain in a state of nature, the haunt of a few wretched savages," the governor would argue before the legislature of the Indiana Territory, "when it seems destined by the Creator to give support to a large population, and to be the sea of civilization, of science, and the true religion?"

The scene of Tecumseh's meeting with Harrison was Vincennes, then a scruffy frontier village on the Wabash River. The Shawnee Indians were surrounded by enemies—hostile settlers, predatory land speculators, acquiescent chiefs, rough soldiers who stood ready to deal with what they perceived as Indian impudence. As Tecumseh prepared to speak, their animosity was palpable, as was their certainty of history's tide: Already, more than 700,000 whites lived in the Old Northwest, outnumbering the 50,000 Indians by better than 10 to one.

The Shawnee began his speech with a litany of wrongs his people had suffered at the hands of the whites. Then he turned to Governor Harrison's recent land grab. In Tecumseh's mind, the deal had no validity. He had come to believe that all Indian lands were a jointly held inheritance. The forests and prairies of the Old Northwest belonged to all tribes living there, he said, and none could sell on their own—which meant, in effect, that the land could never be sold. "No tribe has a right to sell," Tecumseh thundered at one point, "even to each other, much less to strangers, who demand all, and will take no less. Sell a country! Why not sell the air, the clouds, and the great sea, as well as the earth? Did not the Great Spirit make them all for the use of his children?" Tecumseh concluded with an argument the Americans could scarcely refute. The former colonialists, he said, had "set the example of forming a union among all the fires [states]. Why then should they censure the Indians for following it?"

The morning after one particularly angry session, he and Harrison sat down side by side on a bench and talked directly. As legend has it, Tecumseh kept edging along the bench as the conversation continued, gradually forcing the governor toward one end. Just as Harrison was

Little Turtle, a Miami warrior and principal war chief for several allied tribes of the Old Northwest, earned respect for soundly defeating two U.S. Army generals, Josiah Harmar and Arthur St. Clair.

The southern Great Lakes region and Ohio country were the scene of many clashes between whites and Indians following the Revolution. The map at right shows the locations of the tribes, the key white settlements, and the main battle sites. The final resistance, led by Tecumseh, ended with an Indian defeat at the Thames River in Ontario on October 5, 1813.

FT. MICHILIMACKINAC

GEORGIAN BAY

MENOMINEE

LAKE HURON

ONTARIO

MISSISSAUGA

LAKE ONTARIO

FT. NIAGARA

MICHIGAN TERRITORY (1805)

OJIBWA

OTTAWA

LAKE MICHIGAN

WINNEBAGO

NEW YORK

SENECA

Thames River

Moraviantown

THAMES

Detroit
FT. DETROIT

Monquagon

Detroit River

Amherstburg

Raisin River

LAKE ERIE

Allegheny River

RAISIN RIVER

Chicago
FT. DEARBORN

POTAWATOMI

OTTAWA

FALLEN TIMBERS

SENECA

Tippecanoe River

Maumee River

HARMAR'S DEFEAT

FT. MEIGS

FT. STEPHENSON

Youngstown

PENNSYLVANIA

KICKAPOO

FT. WAYNE

SHAWNEE

WYANDOT

Sandusky R.

OHIO (1803)

TIPPECANOE

MIAMI

ST. CLAIR'S DEFEAT

Wheeling

Prophet's Town

WEA

DELAWARE

Greenville

Springfield

Zanesville

Old Piqua

ILLINOIS TERRITORY (1809)

Wabash River

FT. HARRISON

Miami River

Chillicothe

Old Chillicothe

INDIANA TERRITORY (1800)

Cincinnati

FT. WASHINGTON

Point Pleasant

Vincennes

VIRGINIA

DELAWARE

Frankfort

SHAWNEE

Boonesboro

Ohio River

Kentucky River

KENTUCKY (1792)

Cumberland

NORTH CAROLINA

River

BUCHANAN'S STATION

Nashville

CHEROKEE

TENNESSEE (1796)

Scale of Miles

0   25   50   75   100

about to be pushed off, he protested. Tecumseh laughed. That was exactly what the Americans were doing to the Indians, he said.

Although Tecumseh failed to change Harrison's plans, his sweeping vision and implacable will left a profound impression. When Harrison described the conference to his superiors, he likened the charismatic Shawnee to an Indian Moses. The two men would remain adversaries to the end, but the governor never hesitated to acknowledge Tecumseh's greatness. In a letter to William Eustis, President James Madison's secretary of war, Harrison wrote: "The implicit obedience and respect that the followers of Tecumseh pay to him is really astonishing and more than any other circumstance bespeaks him one of those uncommon geniuses, who spring up occasionally to overturn the established order of things. If it were not for the vicinity of the United States, he would perhaps be the founder of an empire that would rival in glory that of Mexico or Peru."

Tecumseh sought no such glory. For this Indian Moses, the Promised Land was already in hand. The challenge was to keep it, whether by words or by guns. He would be the central figure in the long struggle for Indian freedom in the Old Northwest, which began with Pontiac's rebellion in 1763 and ended in 1832 with the defeat of Black Hawk.

The original home of the Shawnee, an Algonquian-speaking people, was probably the Ohio River valley, but their history includes many migrations. During the 17th and 18th centuries, some Shawnee bands lived on lands that are today parts of Kentucky and Tennessee; others settled in western Pennsylvania, Virginia, Maryland, and New York, as well as in the northern parts of South Carolina, Georgia, and Alabama. Tecumseh's father, a war chief named Puckeshinwa, was born in Florida; his mother may have been a Creek. But by the 1760s, most of the Shawnees, about 3,000 in all, had regathered north of the Ohio River in the Old Northwest, although the men still roved far afield during the hunting season.

In 1763, after victory in the French and Indian War, the British prohibited white settlement west of a line running along the crest of the Appalachians. The policy was elegantly simple: Colonists would cultivate and develop the coastal and Piedmont regions, while the Crown reserved the lands beyond the mountains for the Indian fur trade. Within a few years, however, colonial surveyors were roving the trans-Appalachian region, staking out vast tracts for wealthy speculators. Meanwhile, penniless

Scotch-Irish immigrants and other newcomers, who could not afford to buy farmland in the East, flooded across the mountains. The land grabbing sparked conflict with the Indians all along the frontier.

In the fall of 1768, recognizing the reality of the illegal settlements, the British decided to push the territory reserved for the Indians much farther west by negotiating a new boundary with their old allies, the Iroquois. By treating the Six Nations as if they were the rulers of all the Indians of the Old Northwest, the British were able to ignore the rights of other tribes, including the Shawnee. In the resulting Treaty of Fort Stanwix, the Iroquois signed away to the British hundreds of thousands of acres of traditional Shawnee hunting grounds.

Earlier in 1768, between the time of the Mouse-Eared Oaks and the Singing Frogs—as the Shawnee kept track of the year—Tecumseh was born at Old Piqua, a Shawnee village along the Mad River in western Ohio. He was the fifth of eight children. Two older brothers would distinguish themselves as warriors and provide inspiration for Tecumseh. Far more important to his destiny, however, was a younger brother named Lalawethika, or the Noisemaker. This sibling was as awkward and corpulent as Tecumseh was lithe and athletic; he lost an eye in a childhood accident and never mastered the skills of hunting and fighting. As a result, he was treated with contempt by his warrior peers. But one day Lalawethika would remake himself as a holy man and preach a message that would resonate all the way to the White House.

In late 1774, when he was only six years old, Tecumseh suffered a tragic loss. His father, Puckeshinwa, who had fought the British during Pontiac's rebellion a decade earlier, was killed by a band of frontiersmen on the banks of the Ohio River. Puckeshinwa had only recently returned to his family after fighting beside Cornstalk, the great Shawnee war chief, during the struggle known as Lord Dunmore's War, named for an arrogant British governor of Virginia who had reneged on the agreements banning white settlement west of the Appalachians. Although the Shawnee inflicted heavy casualties, they were unable to drive out the settlers and, in the end, lost a decisive battle at Point Pleasant in western Virginia. Against the will of many of his tribesmen, Cornstalk signed a new treaty, yielding still more land. Three years later, Cornstalk, his son, and several Shawnee warriors were murdered by whites in retaliation for the death of a settler at the hands of an unknown Indian. The murders of his father and Cornstalk left Tecumseh alienated from the whites.

Meanwhile, the whites began fighting among themselves. The Revo-

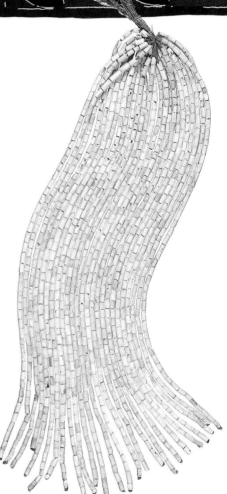

This composite sketch of Tecumseh is based on two drawings, one by Pierre Le Dru, a 19th-century Creole trader, and another by an unnamed British officer. His headdress is a Shawnee specialty, a turban fashioned of trade cloth and decorated with an eagle feather.

lutionary War had erupted. Many Shawnees wanted to remain neutral. But after the death of Cornstalk, the tribe decided to side with the British. After all, it had been the Crown that had guaranteed the Shawnee a territory of their own. The land-hungry colonists, on the other hand, had been the ones who had repeatedly violated agreements with the Indians.

Tecumseh began tagging along with war parties at the age of 14, and he soon showed himself to be a daring warrior: In 1783 he was in the forefront of an attack on flatboats carrying supplies down the Ohio River. But nothing seemed to stop the Americans, especially after they had won their independence. George Washington favored giving cheap or free land grants to Revolutionary War veterans; he expected that they would serve as an excellent militia and that their clearance of the land and reduction of game would discourage the Indians, making them, in his words, "as eager to sell as we are to buy." As government agents began to acquire tracts north of the Ohio River through a series of dubious treaties signed by chiefs who often had no legitimate claim to the land, Tecumseh took up the life of a guerrilla. Full grown now, he was a handsome, powerfully built man, about five feet 10 inches tall. In 1787 he headed south to raid white settlements in the old hunting grounds of Kentucky and Tennessee in retaliation for the destruction of several Shawnee villages. When he returned to the Ohio country in 1790, he was a master of the arts of war and the leader of his band.

While Tecumseh was fighting in the south, bands of Shawnees and Miamis had begun harassing white intruders in the Ohio Valley. After perfunctory efforts to negotiate a compromise, the bellicose Arthur St. Clair,

governor of the Northwest Territory, dispatched General Josiah Harmar to humble "the savages." On September 30, 1790, Harmar set out from Fort Washington, on the site of present-day Cincinnati, with a force of 320 regulars and 1,133 Pennsylvania and Kentucky militiamen. The Americans had not been in the field more than three weeks before they suffered two disastrous ambushes, losing a total of 183 soldiers to a coalition of tribes led by two war chiefs, Little Turtle, a Miami, and Blue Jacket, a Shawnee. Although Tecumseh apparently arrived too late to participate, he did not have to wait long for a fresh opportunity to fight.

Financed by a $300,000 congressional appropriation, St. Clair assembled a force composed of 2,300 militiamen and volunteers, and the following September personally led an expedition into the Maumee Valley. But most of his men were poorly trained. Discouraged by the cold, wet weather, almost half of them deserted after only a few weeks in the field. Meanwhile, more than 1,000 warriors, led by Little Turtle, Blue Jacket, and a Delaware war chief named Buckongahelos, gathered to meet them. The Indians had been alerted to St. Clair's plan by the British, who despite American independence still occupied forts in the Old Northwest and maintained a thriving fur trade. Indian scouts—among them Tecumseh—shadowed St. Clair's army as it blundered across southwestern Ohio. After dark on November 3, the Indians quietly surrounded St. Clair's camp. At dawn they attacked, shouting war whoops that survivors later likened to the howling of wolves. The Indians killed more than 600 Americans and wounded hundreds more. The remnants of St. Clair's force, including the general, scurried back to Fort Washington, arriving on November 9; they covered in five days the same distance it

Possessions attributed to Tecumseh include two gifts from the British: a council belt commemorating the defeat of the French and wampum beads presented by Matthew Elliott, head of the British Indian department during the War of 1812. Also pictured is Tecumseh's 300-pound iron strongbox in which he stored jewelry, documents, and decorations.

had taken them five weeks to traverse during their advance. The debacle remains one of the most lopsided defeats in U.S. military annals.

The crushing reverse stunned the American public and put a temporary halt to western expansion. President Washington ordered his agents to make peace overtures. Federal commissioners, negotiating through Iroquois and British agents, offered to abandon most of their military posts north of the Ohio River, pay $50,000 in trade goods and an annuity of $10,000, and recognize Indian control over most of the Ohio country if the tribes would only relinquish some lands around Cincinnati and the Scioto and the Muskingum rivers. But the Shawnee remained intransigent. They countered by suggesting that the United States government use the funds that it was offering them to pay for the resettlement of the white settlers who were squatting on Indian lands.

Meanwhile, President Washington was also rebuilding the shattered U.S. Army. After the St. Clair debacle, he asked Congress for an even greater outlay—this time, more than $1,000,000—and raised the number of regular soldiers to 5,000. More important, Washington chose an energetic commander in chief, Major General Anthony Wayne, who had the colorful nickname of Mad Anthony. Wayne had served at Valley Forge and Yorktown and earned a reputation as a disciplinarian. While federal agents negotiated with the Indians, Wayne spent two years toughening his force, which became known as the Legion of the United States. When the negotiations collapsed, Washington ordered him to begin ''vigorous offensive action.'' In October 1793, Wayne began moving into the field, building forts at strategic sites and stockpiling ammunition. Among his aides was Tecumseh's future nemesis, William Henry Harrison.

When Tecumseh returned from a second trip south where he lost a brother, Cheeseekau, fighting settlers, he found that Little Turtle was now counseling peace. The great Miami war chief recognized that the whites would keep on coming no matter how many times they were defeated, and he wanted to save Indian lives. But Turkey Foot, another Miami chief, argued for war. Blue Jacket and the Shawnee were also ready to fight. As Wayne approached, Blue Jacket ordered the Shawnee villages along the Maumee River evacuated. He sent the women and children to safety in present-day Michigan and decided to make a stand in a clearing along the river in northwestern Ohio; because the ground was strewn with trees felled by a storm, the place would become known as Fallen Timbers. The site was only five miles upstream from Fort Miami, a redoubt newly built by the British. Blue Jacket hoped to seek help there should the need arise.

Blue Jacket's force of 1,300 warriors—mainly Shawnee and Delaware—was outnumbered by Wayne's legion by almost three to one. By now, the Shawnee had adopted their own nickname for Mad Anthony. They called him Sukachgook, or Black Snake, because of the relentless manner in which he pursued them.

On August 20, 1794, the showdown finally occurred. The fighting began when a band of Shawnees ambushed Wayne's vanguard. But this time the Americans did not panic. Instead, they regrouped and attacked. While Wayne's sharpshooters kept the Indians pinned down, the infantry and cavalry charged. After one frenzied hour, the fighting was over. "We could not stand against the sharp end of their guns," one of the Indians later said, "and we ran to the river, swamps, thickets, and to the islands in the river covered with corn. Our moccasins trickled blood in the sand, and the water was red in the river." Tecumseh and some of the Shawnees were surrounded at one point. Only by a desperate counterattack were they able to break out, but Tecumseh's remaining older brother, Sauwauseekau, was killed. The Indians fled to Fort Miami only to be turned away by their erstwhile British allies, who feared antagonizing the Americans. The Indians then continued their retreat to the shores of Lake Erie, while the victorious Wayne headed back up the Maumee, burning every Indian village he came across.

After the defeat at Fallen Timbers, Tecumseh refused to have anything to do with the peace negotiations that followed in the spring. Those talks, which were held at Wayne's Greenville headquarters in western Ohio, called for the Indians to sign over about two-thirds of the Ohio country, including the ancestral homes of two of the five Shawnee groups. In addition, they would have to surrender a portion of southeastern Indiana and 16 strategic sites across the northern rim of the Old Northwest. In return, the Americans offered $20,000 in trade goods, a modest annuity, and permission to hunt in the ceded territory. In August 1795, one year after the Battle of Fallen Timbers, 91 chiefs from 12 tribes of the Old Northwest affixed their marks on the Treaty of Greenville. Among them were Little Turtle and Blue Jacket, who accepted special gifts and annuities from the Americans. Of the principal Indian war leaders, only Tecumseh elected to remain on the warrior's path.

In 1803 part of the region became the state of Ohio. The Old Northwest was filling up with settlers. That same year, President Thomas Jefferson detailed the government's Indian policy in a letter to William Henry Harrison, who had resigned from the army to hold various administrative

posts in the Northwest Territory. The plan, Jefferson wrote, was to convert the Indians to agriculture: "When they withdraw themselves to the culture of a small piece of land, they will perceive how useless to them are their extensive forests, and will be willing to pare them off from time to time in exchange for necessaries for their farms and families. To promote this disposition, we shall push our trading houses and be glad to see the good and influential individuals among them run in debt, because we observe that when these debts get beyond what the individuals can pay, they become willing to lop them off by a cession of lands."

The policy worked wonders. By 1806 Harrison had induced various tribes to give up 70 million additional acres, all of them west of the supposedly inviolable border set by the Treaty of Greenville. As for converting the tribes to the white man's way of life, however, results were decidedly mixed. Some Shawnees, under the leadership of Black Hoof, set up a farming community in the Auglaize Valley with the help of the U.S. government and Quaker missionaries. But most refused to give up their traditional ways.

Major General Anthony Wayne's mounted recruits clash with the outnumbered Shawnee and Delaware forces led by the war chief Blue Jacket at the Battle of Fallen Timbers in 1794.

The Shawnee culture was in crisis. The land was overhunted; the introduction of woven fabrics, metal tools, and other trade goods had extinguished ancient crafts; smallpox, whooping cough, influenza, venereal diseases, and alcoholism were taking a grievous toll. Most frontier whites considered the Indians savages and wanted them exterminated. Indians seeking trade were often murdered by frontier ruffians. Under the cultural onslaught, the tribes of the Old Northwest began to wither away.

Tecumseh's band now numbered some 100 Shawnees, and his name

was respected throughout the region. But he was not yet ready to claim leadership. It would take the transformation of his younger brother to carry Tecumseh to the center of events on the frontier.

For the better part of his life, Lalawethika was the polar opposite of Tecumseh: lazy, boastful, and a hard drinker. But in 1805, during an epidemic, he fell into a series of trances and emerged fundamentally changed. While he was unconscious, he said, two young men had carried him into the spirit world, where he met the supreme deity, the Master of Life, who showed him a paradise of game-rich forests and fertile cornfields—the way the earth was before the whites spoiled it. The Master of Life told him that the paradise could become a reality if the Shawnee would follow a path of virtue.

Lalawethika spelled out the requirements. He had heard the Master of Life say: "The Americans I did not make. They are not my children, but the children of the Evil Spirit." According to his vision, the white race had been created on the shores of North America by malevolent powers residing either in a giant crab or in the scum that washes onto the beaches. He besought his people to stop imitating the whites and to embrace their own culture. Accumulated wealth and private property, for example, were vices of the selfish white man. Warriors must again devote themselves to caring for the needy and the elderly. Instead of hoarding possessions, they should give away their wealth in the traditional manner. They must cease quarreling with each other, abstain from alcohol, and refuse to prostitute their wives and daughters. The Shawnee must again rely on wild game and native crops for food, dress in animal skins, and make their implements from natural materials such as stone or wood (although firearms were permissible for self-defense). If all the instructions were obeyed, said Lalawethika, the Master of Life had promised: ''I will overturn the land, so that all the white people will be covered and you alone shall inhabit the land.''

Lalawethika enjoyed exceptional success. Renaming himself Tenskwatawa, or the Open Door, he ordered the old medicine bundles discarded. To replace them, he created new sacred objects, including strings of holy beads similar to rosaries. He also created new rituals. He asked the Shawnee to extinguish their old lodge fires and light new ones, using Indian bow drills and natural tinder instead of the white man's flint and steel. The new religion found many disciples.

The most illustrious convert was Tecumseh. When the Prophet established a camp for believers in western Ohio at Greenville on the site of a decommissioned fort, Tecumseh moved there. Over the next two years, as word of the Indian messiah spread, the camp grew. To their chagrin, American officials inadvertently contributed to the movement's success. Governor William Henry Harrison, attempting to use scorn as a weapon, suggested to Tenskwatawa's followers that they ask the Prophet to prove his power by performing a miracle. Somehow—possibly from British agents—Tenskwatawa learned of an imminent solar eclipse. As an enormous throng in Greenville watched on June 16, 1806, he pointed commandingly at the sun shortly before noon, and the moon slowly covered it. Then, summoning the power of the Master of Life, he brought the sun back. The feat created a sensation.

The Americans also boosted the movement by continuing to take Indian lands. But Tenskwatawa did not concern himself much with such issues, preferring a role as a religious

A detail from a George Catlin portrait shows Tenskwatawa, Tecumseh's younger brother and spiritual adviser, in traditional dress. Unlike Tecumseh, the Shawnee prophet cut no striking figure; he was ungainly, and blind in one eye.

instructor. Tecumseh stepped forward as the political leader. This role required him to engage in a dialogue with the Americans, and although he had often resisted dealing with them in the past, he did not stint now.

Tecumseh realized that the only hope of halting the whites was to persuade the tribes to combine their strength. A first step in that direction was to move the center of the religious movement westward, closer to the tribes of present-day Illinois and Michigan, which had been particularly responsive to Tenskwatawa's preaching. In 1807 the two brothers shifted their camp to a site provided by Main Poc, a Potawatomi war chief and shaman. The new village, called Prophet's Town, lay close to the juncture of the Tippecanoe and Wabash rivers.

As the followers of Tenskwatawa put up their wigwams, Tecumseh traveled to Canada to meet with the British. He recognized that the Indians needed the support of the redcoats if they were to defend their lands; he also was aware of increasing tensions between Great Britain and the United States, and that war between the two white powers was a possibility. The British were much impressed by Tecumseh—one official described him as a "shrewd intelligent man"—and they favored an alliance with the tribes if war did break out.

Tecumseh spent the winter of 1808–1809 traveling among the Wyandot and Seneca. He had only limited success with them, but that spring he gained many recruits farther west, among the Winnebago and among the bands of Sauk and Fox led by the war chief Black Hawk, who would later kindle a resistance movement of his own.

By now, Tecumseh was the real leader of the movement. The following summer, he challenged William Henry Harrison at Vincennes. The Indian demonstrated the plight of his people by inching Harrison toward the end of a bench. And he wove a spell of words, warning that he had "organized a combination of all the Indian tribes in this quarter to put a stop to the encroachments of the white people" and that any attempt to survey the fraudulently sold lands would trigger war. Finally, stunning his listeners, he declared, "I am alone the acknowledged head of all the Indians." He was not—Black Hoof, for example, denounced Tecumseh. But the statement had a nightmare ring to the officials at Vincennes. Tecumseh knew that the idea of a pantribal leader was anathema to the Americans and would invite their most hostile attentions. Thenceforth, welding the Indians into an effective confederacy became his supreme goal.

That winter, Tecumseh again ventured to Canada and sat in council with the British as the principal spokesman for a large contingent of Potawatomi, Ottawa, Sauk, and Winnebago warriors. In the spring of 1811, he traveled among the tribes of western Michigan and dispatched messengers to tribes farther north and west to convey his message of unity. By summer, his confederacy included most of the tribes of the Old Northwest, but his proselytizing efforts were only beginning. In August he and about 20 warriors trekked south to enlist the Choctaw, Chickasaw, Creek, and others. Tirelessly, in one village after another, Tecumseh stoked the fires of resistance, addressing crowds of several thousand with the help of a Shawnee shaman named Sikaboo, who acted as his translator.

In a few cases, white agents were on hand to record Tecumseh's words. "Where are the Narragansett, the Mahican, the Pokanoket, and many other once powerful tribes of our people?" Tecumseh argued during one debate. "They have vanished before the avarice and oppression of the white man, as snow before a summer sun. Shall we, without a struggle, give up our homes, our country bequeathed to us by the Great Spirit, the graves of our dead and everything that is dear and sacred to us. I know you will cry with me, Never! Never!"

Sam Dale, a white observer, never forgot the sight of the determined warrior, dressed only in moccasins and a breechcloth, face streaked with red war paint. "The words fell in avalanches from his lips," Dale recalled. "His eyes burned with supernatural luster, and his old frame trembled with emotion. His voice resounded over the multitude—now sinking in low and musical whispers, now rising to the highest keys, hurling out his words like a succession of thunderbolts. I have heard many great orators, but I never saw one with the vocal powers of Tecumseh."

Yet the southern chiefs remained cautious. The Choctaw, who had many mixed bloods and had embraced many of the ways of the white man, were especially unreceptive. Only the Creek and Seminole welcomed Tecumseh with enthusiasm.

William Henry Harrison, meanwhile, had concluded that the Shawnee-led deliverance movement was a grave threat to American interests. Shortly after Tecumseh left on his southern mission, the governor expressed his fear in a letter he wrote to William Eustis in Washington. Tecumseh's absence, Harrison noted, "affords a most favorable opportunity for breaking up his confederacy." If the secretary would authorize an attack on Prophet's Town before Tecumseh's return, said Harrison, "then that part of the fabric which he considered complete will be demolished and even its foundations rooted up." Eustis granted the request.

On September 26, 1811, Harrison marched on Prophet's Town. His

force of 1,000 stopped to build a fort near the site of modern Terre Haute. Tenskwatawa and Tecumseh had agreed that the movement needed to bring in the southern tribes before taking on the whites. But with Harrison camped only two miles away, Tenskwatawa felt he could wait no longer. He gave permission for an attack.

It began in the predawn hours of November 7. A force of about 600 Winnebagos, Potawatomis, Kickapoos, and other Indians crept forward under cover of darkness. But a sentry spotted them, and his shot roused the camp. Harrison's men met the Indians with a blizzard of musket fire. After two hours of fighting, the Indians scattered. They blamed Tenskwatawa for their failure and angrily returned to their villages. Harrison then seized 5,000 bushels of corn and beans and burned the deserted Prophet's Town. Soon afterward, he marched home in triumph. In fact, the Battle of Tippecanoe, as it came to be known, was a modest victory, with

The Sauk and Fox, some of whom are shown here dancing around a prisoner dressed in red, were among the many Indian groups that joined the pantribal movement begun by Tecumseh and Tenskwatawa in 1808.

about 60 deaths on both sides. But it gained luster with time and gave Harrison a nickname, memorialized in the slogan Tippecanoe and Tyler, Too, which helped him win the presidency in 1840.

When Tecumseh returned from his trip in January 1812 and discovered what had happened, he was enraged at his brother's recklessness. The Prophet's medicine was broken. In the aftermath of the failed attack, Tenskwatawa lost his following. Now the only hope lay in fighting.

The destruction of Prophet's Town inflamed Indians throughout the Old Northwest, and their wrath was vented in raids against settlers. But these uncoordinated encounters had little effect except to rouse the fury of the Americans. Tecumseh tried to buy time by sending placating messages to Harrison. But both he and the governor saw war coming—a war that would pit the Americans against an alliance of Indians and the British. The full storm broke on June 18, 1812, in good part because of the bloodshed on the frontier.

One aspect of the American plan was obvious: American forces would invade Canada. To the backwoods settlers, it seemed the only solution to the Indian problem. As long as the Indians could find sanctuary north of the border, frontier families would have no peace, or so their legislators argued. For that purpose, the Americans sent a force of 3,000 to Detroit, then a frontier town with a population of about 700. The force was led by 60-year-old Brigadier General William Hull, a Revolutionary War hero. Hull crossed the Detroit River into Ontario on July 12, intending to attack the British fort at Amherstburg. Despite having overwhelming numerical superiority, he dithered, worrying about his lack of artillery. About two weeks later, he learned that a combined British and Indian force had captured an American fort on Michilimackinac Island in the straits that join Lake Huron and Lake Michigan. The fall of the fort and the stalling of Hull's drive signaled American weakness to the regional tribes, and many bands of Wyandots, Ottawas, and Ojibwas that had remained neutral up to that point joined the British. They looked to Tecumseh for leadership. He would not disappoint them.

To aid Hull, American officials in Ohio sent a supply train with a troop of 230 militiamen under a Captain Henry Brush. Hull dispatched a relief column of 150 troops to rendezvous with the convoy at the Raisin River. But Indian scouts tracked the column, and on the morning of August 4, Tecumseh prepared an ambush at a site where the soldiers would have to ford a creek just south of Detroit. He positioned two dozen warriors in heavy underbrush close to the fording point. As the Americans splashed

A print from an 1810 travel account captioned "An Indian and His Squaw" features an ill-clad and downtrodden couple. The man's ragged shirt and the bottle he holds in his left hand signify the decaying social conditions with which Indian leaders had to contend.

across the stream, the Indians opened fire, killing 19 and wounding 12. The survivors fled to Detroit without ever making contact with Brush. Outnumbered by six to one, the Indians suffered only a single fatality.

Hull was unnerved by this action in his rear, and he retreated back across the Detroit River to American soil. A few days later, he sent a larger relief force under Lieutenant Colonel James Miller toward the supply column. Tecumseh's warriors and some British regulars attacked them near Monguagon, a small Wyandot village. Although Miller managed to drive them off, the Americans suffered heavy casualties, and Hull, fearful of yet another ambush, ordered Miller back to Detroit.

During the battle, Tecumseh was hit in the leg with buckshot. Although painful, the wound did not greatly impede him. When he returned to Amherstburg, his spirits were lifted by the arrival of 300 British reinforcements. The troops were led by an officer who immediately struck Tecumseh as a true fighter: Major General Isaac Brock was tall, forceful, and aggressive. He welcomed Tecumseh's suggestion to launch an immediate attack on Detroit and promised victory in an address to the assembled warriors. Brock's speech made a great impression, especially on Tecumseh, who felt that the British had at last sent the Indians a true warrior. Reportedly, the Shawnee turned to a group of bystanders and said in English, "This is a man!"

Brock placed Tecumseh in command of all the Indians, and the counterinvasion began. Before dawn on August 16, Tecumseh and about 600 warriors slipped across the Detroit River and took up positions on the north and west sides of the American settlement. In the hours that followed, they moved in and out of the woods in plain sight: Hull was known to have a dread of Indians, and—by the tactic of allowing him to capture a British courier—he had been fed false information that 5,000 warriors from the upper lakes had joined the British side. When Brock began shelling the fort from the south, Hull, fearing for the safety of the town's women and children, surrendered without a fight.

The capitulation was the high-water mark of Tecumseh's war against the Americans. Thereafter, a general stalemate set in. Ten days after the capture of Detroit, Isaac Brock left for the Niagara region. In October, he was killed in battle. But even if the British had not lost their finest frontier

commander, their prosecution of the war would not have satisfied Tecumseh. British aims were strictly defensive; they were fighting to save Canada, not to drive the Americans from the Old Northwest.

Tecumseh labored tirelessly to hold the confederacy together. In the spring of 1813, he still had more than 1,000 warriors at his disposal, and in late April he joined a British force to again take on Harrison, who had been put in command of America's frontier forces.

As part of a plan to advance methodically, Harrison had built Fort Meigs on the Maumee River not far from the Fallen Timbers battle site. On May 1, the British began a bombardment, and they continued lofting explosive shells. But Harrison's engineers had built a system of earthworks that kept casualties to a minimum. Harrison knew that a brigade of Kentuckians was marching to reinforce him, and he refused to surrender.

A ship sails from Fort Malden on the Detroit River in an 1813 watercolor by Catherine Reynolds, daughter of a British military officer stationed at the outpost. Tecumseh (inset detail), who helped the British capture Detroit in 1812, is in the foreground dressed in feathers and striped military trousers.

The Kentuckians engaged the British and the Indians on May 5—and ran straight into disaster. Tecumseh's warriors pinned the Americans against the Maumee River and cut them to pieces, killing nearly 500 and capturing 150; only 150 managed to reach Fort Meigs. Yet that day of triumph gained little. Although Colonel Henry Procter, Brock's successor, had promised Tecumseh that Harrison would be his personal prisoner, he was unprepared to maintain a siege. Instead he withdrew, taking the American prisoners back to his headquarters. Procter then looked the other way as the Indians began torturing the captives. When Tecumseh arrived, he put a stop to the massacre. Survivors later told of how Tecumseh knocked down several Indians and verbally assaulted Procter for failing to maintain order. Tecumseh had condemned a similar massacre on the Raisin River four months earlier. He realized that if the Indians were ever to gain a state of their own, they would have to make peace with the Americans and be recognized for their humanity on white terms.

In late July, Tecumseh and Procter made another attempt on Fort Meigs, but the post had been strengthened, and they failed again. A few days after this disappointment, they attacked Fort Stephenson, a smaller post on the Sandusky River. But it, too, held. As word of the setbacks spread and Harrison continued to build up his forces, tribes throughout the Old Northwest began to reconsider their alliance with the British. Then came catastrophe. On September 10, 1813, Captain Oliver Hazard Perry, commander of a newly built American fleet on Lake Erie, won a crushing victory over the British fleet, sinking or capturing every vessel.

Tecumseh learned of the debacle nine days later from Procter, who then related more bad news. He informed the assembled officers and Indian leaders that the British had decided to bow to the reality of American strength and retreat. He hoped that Tecumseh and the other Indians would join in the defense of Canada. Tecumseh was stunned. Dressed in buckskin, with an ostrich plume in his hair, he glared at the British commander. Then he began to speak. His words electrified the audience: "Father, listen to your children! Our great father, the king, is our head, and you represent him. You always told us that you would never draw your feet off British ground; but now we see you are drawing back, and we are sorry to see our father doing so without seeing the enemy. We must compare our father's conduct to a fat animal that carries its tail upon its back, but when affrightened, he drops it between his legs and runs off. Father! You have got the arms and ammunition that our great father sent for his red children. If you have an idea of going away, give them to us, and you may go and welcome. As for us, our lives are in the hands of the Great Spirit. We are determined to defend our lands, and if it be his will, we wish to leave our bones upon them."

Procter promised to respond in three days. But the British commander did not dare risk another public confrontation. Instead he met with Tecumseh privately, explaining how the American control of Lake Erie jeopardized British land forces. Tecumseh listened carefully, and the two men worked out a compromise: The British would retreat about 50 miles up the Thames River—beyond the reach of Perry's squadron—and make a stand there if Harrison pursued them.

Tecumseh, dependent on British supplies and matériel, had little choice but to accept this scheme. He tried to convince his Indian allies that the plan was sound. But they continued to drift away, believing that the British had no will to fight. Others, loyal to Tecumseh, including a large number of women and children who had been with him since Prophet's Town, retreated with the British toward the Thames.

On September 27, Harrison and 3,000 troops crossed Lake Erie into Canada. In a desperate effort to slow him down, Tecumseh and his remaining warriors began destroying the bridges over McGregor's Creek, a tributary of the Thames. But in an engagement on October 4, Harrison brushed the Indians aside with artillery. In that encounter, Tecumseh received a slight wound in the left arm.

On October 5 came the showdown. Procter and Tecumseh chose to meet Harrison's army on the north side of the Thames, not far from Moraviantown. The British established their lines across a road where it traversed a swamp; the Indians waited in thickets on either side of the road. Harrison's soldiers forded the Thames and marched toward them. "Father," Tecumseh advised Procter, "tell your men to be firm, and all will be well." But when the forces met in midafternoon, the British collapsed and began retreating toward Moraviantown. Procter, watching from the rear, galloped away. Tecumseh fought on, shouting encouragement. But it was hopeless. Harrison's forces delivered overwhelming firepower into the underbrush. A bullet caught Tecumseh in the chest. The previous night, some of his warriors later recounted, he had calmly said, "My body will remain on the battlefield." Now the light dimmed, and his vision of Indian unity and strength faded with the afternoon sun. The yells and percussion of guns grew distant, then fell silent. The Indian Moses was dead.

Tecumseh's body was never found. It had vanished, along with his farsighted dream. Six years later, the *Indiana Centinel* of Vincennes wrote:

Black Hawk, a Sauk and the last of the great Indian chiefs in the fight for the Old Northwest, wears a traditional roach of animal fur atop his shaved head in this 1833 portrait by Charles Bird King. Before the Sauk obtained scissors in trade, they plucked their hair, removed it with sharp blades, or burned it off with hot stones, a long and painful ordeal.

"Every schoolboy in the Union now knows that Tecumseh was a great man. He was truly great—and his greatness was his own, unassisted by science or the aids of education. As a statesman, a warrior, and a patriot, take him all in all, we shall not look upon his like again." Tecumseh's hold on the American imagination of the time was unparalleled. There were tales of his humanity, his nobility, his wisdom, even of a romance with a young white woman. But the white man's title of Greatest Indian or Red Napoleon provided no consolation to his people. Just as Tecumseh had foreseen, the forces of history pushed the Indians of the Old Northwest farther and farther away from their ancestral lands. The Shawnee eventually landed west of the Mississippi. With them went Tecumseh's brother, Tenskwatawa, the former Prophet, who became in his old age a bit of a curiosity to white visitors. He died peacefully in 1837.

The Old Northwest never saw another Indian leader like Tecumseh. But there were other notable chiefs who would rather die than yield their lands. Among them was a one-time ally of Tecumseh, Makataimeshekia-

This portrait of Black Hawk (right) and his son Whirling Thunder was painted in 1833 while the two were being held prisoner. They were treated more like celebrities than captives; admirers sent gifts, and several women tried to kiss Whirling Thunder, who was described as a "noble specimen of physical beauty."

kiak, or Black Hawk, leader of a band of Sauk Indians, an Algonquian-speaking people whose name derives from a word meaning Yellow Earth People. In 1832, almost two decades after Tecumseh's death, Black Hawk led the last valiant spasm of Indian resistance in the Old Northwest, a warrior's farewell known to history as the Black Hawk War.

Black Hawk was born in 1767, one year before Tecumseh, in the village of Saukenuk, on the present-day site of Rock Island, Illinois, where the Rock River flows into the Mississippi. Three decades before his birth, the Sauk, who numbered about 4,500, allied with the Mesquakie, or Red Earth People. Known to whites as the Fox, they totaled about 1,600. The Fox had settled on the nearby lower Wisconsin River. Both tribes had migrated to the Illinois-southern Wisconsin area as a result of pressures exerted by the 17th-century wars between the Great Lakes Algonquians and the Iroquois. In 1769 Sauk and Fox warriors gained complete control of the surrounding tall-grass prairies and wooded river valleys by displacing and nearly annihilating the original occupants, the Illinois Indians, for whom the state was later named.

The Sauk and Fox shared much in common. Both understood the world to be filled with good and evil spirits that could be summoned through dreams and visions. Black Hawk's totem, for example, was the sparrow hawk, and he hung its medicine skin from his waist in order to share in the raptor's power. The Sauk and Fox also had similar political systems, with older civil chiefs overseeing the communities in times of peace and proven warriors providing leadership in times of war.

The lives of the Sauk and Fox followed a regular cycle. In spring and summer, they lived in villages of large bark-covered dwellings, and grew corn and other vegetables in garden plots along the riverbanks. After the fall harvest, they divided into bands, traveling far and wide by canoe or on horseback to hunt, fish, and trap. When the severe winter weather arrived, they pitched their reed-covered wigwams and remained in place until the warming rays of the spring sun told them that it was time to return to their villages to plant the next year's crops.

The Sauk and Fox had no warning that their world was threatened until 1803, when the United States bought the Louisiana Territory from France and sent a detail of troops to Saint Louis to stake claim to the land. Not long afterward, a few Sauks killed three newly arrived settlers. William Henry Harrison was ordered to bring the Indian killers to justice. In response to a letter from Harrison, the Sauk and Fox sent a delegation of civil chiefs to Saint Louis in September 1804. With them was one of the

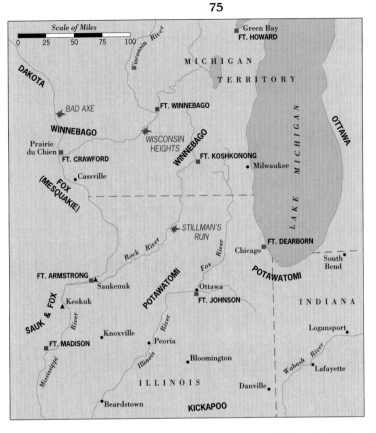

The fertile banks of the Rock River near present-day Rock Island, Illinois, served as farmland for the Sauk and Fox before the tribe was forced to migrate farther west during the 1830s.

Territorial disputes between the Americans and the Sauk and Fox led to the Black Hawk War of 1832, the last of the conflicts for the Old Northwest. Black Hawk and his band met the federal forces at Stillman's Run and the Wisconsin River. The Indians were eventually defeated at the Battle of the Bad Axe.

warriors involved in the quarrel with the settlers. In accordance with Indian custom, the chiefs gave the whites some goods "to wipe away the tears" of the relatives of the dead men and also surrendered the warrior, expecting the whites to reciprocate, Indian fashion, by releasing him. Instead, Harrison insisted that the chiefs had to buy his freedom by selling land. After plying them with liquor, Harrison talked the chiefs into signing a treaty ceding all of their lands on the east side of the Mississippi as well as sizable tracts on the west. The cession included Saukenuk, center of the Sauk world. To add insult to injury, the whites never released the Sauk warrior; instead, they shot him, allegedly while he was attempting to escape.

To the extent that the Sauk grasped the legal proceedings at all, they believed that they were simply sharing their hunting grounds. When they realized that the Americans not only intended to settle their land but also had killed their fellow tribesman who had given himself up in good faith, they were deeply embittered—none more so than Black Hawk. As white settlement drew closer, he sought some way of reversing the slide toward dispossession. For a time, his hopes centered on the mystical movement founded by Tenskwatawa; he responded to its anti-American message and during the War of 1812 joined Tecumseh in a number of battles.

Not all of the Sauk and Fox were willing to fight, however. With their homeland caught between the warring forces, many of them felt threatened by both sides. Some bands yielded to American promises of safety by moving west of the Mississippi River. The migration drove a wedge through the nation. Among those arguing to remain at Saukenuk was a skilled orator in his thirties named Keokuk, or One Who Moves About Alert. Although Keokuk had never killed an enemy and thus did not qualify as a warrior, the band of warriors who had remained at Saukenuk selected him as their new war chief because of his way with words.

Meanwhile, Black Hawk continued to enhance his warrior's reputa-

tion. In July 1814, he led a Sauk and Fox force that drove off a large body of Americans sent to build a fort at Prairie du Chien. In retaliation, Major Zachary Taylor—another future president—sailed up the Mississippi with 430 troops bent on wiping out the Indian villages. Black Hawk met him with more than 1,000 warriors. With the help of a three-pounder gun and an artillery crew sent by the British, Black Hawk won another victory, eventually driving Taylor back to Saint Louis.

With his warriors unbeaten on the battlefield, Black Hawk was shocked in 1815 to hear of the Treaty of Ghent, the peace agreement between the United States and Great Britain. "I have fought the Big Knives and will continue to fight them till they are off our lands," he told a British general. But with the British retreat, his hopes of victory were doomed.

In 1816 Black Hawk and Keokuk traveled with the civil chiefs to Saint Louis, where the Sauk and Fox leaders reluctantly reconfirmed the treaty of 1804 and agreed never to reunite the Rock River bands and the bands now living west of the Mississippi. The peace that ensued was short-lived, however. As more settlers entered the area, the game animals fled. In order to feed their starving families, Sauk and Fox hunters found it necessary to travel north and west into the Sioux hunting grounds. Intertribal fighting broke

out. When a few settlers were killed in the turmoil, the Americans blamed the Sauk and Fox. In this time of crisis, Keokuk argued for friendship with the Americans, who in turn accorded him attention that steadily raised his prestige. In 1824 Keokuk, now a civil chief, led a delegation to

A wooden bowl (opposite) carved from the root of a walnut tree is believed to have been among Black Hawk's personal possessions. The Sauk chief is said to have presented Jonah Case, an early white settler, with the ceremonial pipe tomahawk above as a token of esteem. The pipe shown below, adorned with beads and animal fur, was crafted by Black Hawk himself while he was a prisoner of the United States government.

Washington, where he signed away more Sauk land. Black Hawk was incensed. He called Keokuk a coward and a traitor.

Black Hawk had watched the strength of the Americans burgeon, and he was under no illusions about defeating them. Considering that the odds would only grow longer, he was willing to give up some territory in return for rights to the Sauk heartland. But the whites saw no need for deal making. In 1828 federal officials announced that settlers were coming to take over; the Sauk and Fox would have to be gone by spring.

Keokuk accepted the decree and led part of the tribe to a new village on the Iowa River. But Black Hawk refused to leave. Saukenuk would forever be his home. Later he would explain his feelings: "It was here that I was born, and here lie the bones of many friends and relations. For this spot, I felt a sacred reverence, and never could consent to leave it."

That fall, when the Sauk were away hunting, white squatters took over part of Saukenuk. Black Hawk did not try to evict them when he and his followers returned; they just moved into lodges that were still empty. In July 1829, the government put the land in and around Saukenuk up for public sale. Black Hawk ignored the action. He returned as usual after the hunting season, even though settlers had now enclosed most of the fields around the village with fences, and cattle ranged across whatever open land was left. But Black Hawk refused to bend. When he left to hunt in the fall, he promised that his band would be back the next spring. He was as good as his word.

The federal government responded with an ultimatum. Its representative, General Edmund P. Gaines, traveled to Saukenuk to meet with tribal leaders. When Black Hawk and his die-hards arrived painted for war, Gaines coldly informed them that he was there to enforce the treaty of 1804 and that the Sauk could either move across the Mississippi voluntarily or be driven across at bayonet point. Keokuk supported Gaines, claiming the Americans were too powerful to resist. There were already 150,000 of them in Illinois. But Black Hawk remained adamant.

This portrait of White Cloud, Black Hawk's confidant and spiritual adviser, was painted in 1832 by George Catlin. According to the artist, the Winnebago prophet was letting his hair grow long at the time to gain an advantage with the whites.

The Sauk war chief looked for help from other tribes. The previous year, he had even sent one of his sons to the Osage, the Sauk's traditional enemy, to propose an alliance. But the Osage were not interested. Now he turned to the Kickapoo and Potawatomi, and to the Winnebago followers of White Cloud, a fiercely anti-American holy man. When Gaines learned that the Winnebago prophet had visited Black Hawk, he decided to launch a preemptive strike on Saukenuk. At dawn on June 26, 1831, federal troops and militiamen attacked the village. But Black Hawk was a step ahead; during the night, he and his people had crossed the Mississippi to safety. Gaines ordered Saukenuk burned to the ground.

The next day, Gaines sent messengers to summon Black Hawk to a peace conference. Now deeply concerned about his group's lack of food supplies, Black Hawk returned and finally compromised. He signed a humiliating agreement promising never to return to Saukenuk and to henceforth recognize Keokuk as the Sauk leader. In exchange, Gaines agreed to provide Black Hawk's band with enough corn to survive the winter—a promise the settlers had no intention of keeping.

Black Hawk and his followers, including White Cloud (far left), are shown as they were incarcerated at Jefferson Barracks in 1832. The group refused to cooperate with artist George Catlin until he agreed to depict them wearing their detested balls and chains.

Black Hawk was now almost 65 years old. He expected to die soon, and the Americans had assured him he could be buried in Saukenuk beside his ancestors. But the warrior in him still endured. One month after he had accepted Gaines's terms, a band of Fox warriors killed a number of Menominees and Sioux in a retaliatory raid. The massacre aroused the settlers, who feared another uprising. The whites badgered the government to arrest the perpetrators. When the Fox warriors came to Black Hawk for advice, he praised them for asserting their Indian principles. Revenge was part of the Sauk and Fox culture, and a dispute between tribes was none of the Americans' business.

In early 1832, Black Hawk headed back to Saukenuk for the planting season. With him were almost 2,000 men, women, and children from various tribes. Government officials, warned of his plans to return by Keokuk, sent a large force of regular troops and Illinois volunteers to intercept him (one volunteer was 23-year-old Abraham Lincoln). A series of bloody engagements ensued, as the Americans chased Black Hawk into Wisconsin. The Indians hid in marshes there, slowly starving, and by

Keokuk, Black Hawk's rival who was recognized as chief by federal officials, was not known for his prowess in war but boasted all the trappings of a warrior, including a roach, shield, lance, tomahawk, and bear-claw necklace. Artist George Catlin noted his subject's vanity, recalling that "he brought all his costly wardrobe" to pose for this portrait.

summer, Black Hawk had finally accepted that he would never see Saukenuk again. He decided to throw in his lot with the rest of the Sauk nation in Iowa and spend his last years in peace.

But for his beleaguered band, the way west would prove tragically elusive. On July 21, as they attempted to cross the Wisconsin River, they were detected by U.S. Army scouts. A firefight erupted, and as many as 40 warriors were cut down. Some of the old men, women, and children fled downstream; few got far. Black Hawk and the rest of the band made it across the Wisconsin and pushed westward toward the Mississippi. When they reached the great river on August 1, they fashioned rafts and prepared to make the crossing. Just then, a steamboat carrying soldiers and an artillery piece swept down on them. Black Hawk tried to raise a white flag, but the soldiers fired shells into their midst, killing 23 before the Indians were able to scramble to safety.

By then, the number of Black Hawk's followers had dwindled to fewer than 500. In a council that night, he recommended that they make their way north to seek refuge among the Ojibwa. But the majority of the Indians rejected the idea, believing that they would be safe only if they managed to get across the river. Their decision brought on the last tragic act in the bloody drama—but Black Hawk would not witness it. He and 50 others headed north that night, leaving the main body of the group on the banks of the Mississippi.

The Americans attacked shortly before dawn. It was a massacre. The soldiers shot and clubbed the Indians as they attempted to find cover on the boggy shore. They picked off women and children who plunged into the river. Some Indians managed to swim to several small islands, but the steamer returned and swept the islands with artillery fire. A fraction of the band made it all the way across the river. But awaiting them there were the Sioux, who had entered the hunt for Black Hawk at the government's request. As 68 fleeing warriors struggled to seeming safety on the far shore, the Sioux killed them one by one.

The full toll of that long day will never be known with certainty; between 150 and 300 Indians died. As for Black Hawk, he surrendered in mid-August and was sent off to prison. He was soon released, but government officials saw to it that the Sauk paid heavily for his rebellion. In September of 1832, they proclaimed Keokuk head chief. They then claimed the spoils of victory in a new treaty. The Sauk gave up a strip of land some 50 miles wide on the Iowa side of the Mississippi—six million acres of some of the richest soil in the world. ◄◊►

TOURING THE CAPITAL

When the Winnebago chief Hoowaneka visited John Quincy Adams's White House in 1828, he thought he had found paradise. "So large and beautiful was the President's House, the carpets, the tables, the mirrors, the chairs, and every article in it," he recalled, "that when I entered it, I thought I was in heaven, and the old man there, I thought was the Great Spirit."

His reaction was just what federal officials hoped for when they invited Indian delegates to Washington, D.C., in the 19th century to impress them with the power and superiority of white civilization—and thereby persuade them to sign treaties and peacefully cede their lands. Chieftains were housed in luxurious accommodations, where they ate and drank the best of everything at government expense. They were plied with ceremonial gifts, such as peace medals and flags, as well as more practical items like tailored suits and tobacco. And every visit featured tours of cultural landmarks: the Capitol, the National Theater, art galleries, and the White House.

Many delegates were awed by the nation's capital. Others, however, were repelled by the white man's devious tactics. Young Man Afraid of His Horses, an Oglala Sioux chief, gave this account of his 1891 visit to Washington: "We had some promises, but they are like all other promises of the Great Father. We are not fooled, and we go home with heavy hearts."

Delegates who traveled east faced hazards other than false promises. For many the trip itself proved unsettling; the white man's monstrous, unnatural contrivances—smoking steamboats and screeching locomotives—inspired fear and distress. Worse, many tribal leaders never made it home again, having contracted fatal diseases such as measles and pneumonia to which they had had no previous exposure. Still other delegates returned home to face the scorn of their brethren who refused to believe fantastic stories about the white man's capital.

In the name of the Chickasaw Nation, and by authority in me vested by Law, I, _Wm L. Byrd_ , Governor of the Chickasaw Nation do this day commission

Hon. Overton Love National _Delegate_

of _the_ , C. N.

In testimony hereof, I have hereunto set my hand and caused the great seal of the Chickasaw Nation to be affixed at Tishomingo, the Capitol of said Nation, this, the 16th day of _January_ 18 90.

Wm L. Byrd
Governor of the C. N.

ATTEST _M. V. Cheadle_
National Secretary C. N.

A document dated January 16, 1890, certifies that Overton Love is an official delegate of the Chickasaw Nation. Such credentials were first issued in the 1830s in response to the problem of Indian groups who presumed to negotiate treaties without securing the prior consent of their tribes.

The earliest known photograph of Indians in Washington, D.C., dated December 31, 1857, features a delegation of Pawnee, Ponca, Potawatomi, and Sauk and Fox men assembled on the South Portico of the White House. The Indian representatives, dressed in buckskin and feathers, stand beside government bureaucrats in coats and top hats.

President Andrew Johnson greets representatives of the Santee, Yankton, and upper Missouri Sioux tribes at a reception held in the East Room of the White House on February 23, 1867.

Andrew Jackson gave this flag to Ojibwa leader She-boy-way in 1836. The government commissioned Philadelphia merchants to make flags for Indian delegates.

A SHOW OF EASTERN HOSPITALITY

Exchanging gifts with the Indians was a centuries-old custom dating back to the arrival of the first Europeans in the New World. The United States government continued the tradition by offering Indian visitors first-class accommodations as well as a variety of tokens, including flags and ornaments, in an effort to gain their allegiance.

Clothing was the most common gift; federal agents reasoned that the quickest way to civilize the Indian was to make him look like a white man. The Indians reciprocated with their own offerings, including buffalo robes, peace pipes, and feathered headdresses. Medicine Bear, a Lakota Sioux, actually removed his own shirt and presented it to a surprised President Ulysses S. Grant at a White House reception in 1872. The chief explained that he wanted the Great Father to have his prized war tunic, complete with scalp locks, "in token of the estimation" in which he held him.

The government's gifts were offered in another spirit, however, one made clear by the statement that accompanied a package of trinkets sent in 1828 to The Little Prince, elderly head chief of the Creek Indians who was unable to travel to the capital. "You will consider these things," the note said, "as fastening one of your hands in the hand of your Great Father, and the hand of the Secretary of War."

Jesse Brown's Indian Queen Hotel, located on Pennsylvania Avenue about halfway between the Capitol and the White House, was the accommodation of choice for Indian visitors during the 1820s. According to proprietor Brown, the establishment was a "large and spacious building" unsurpassed "by any hotel in the District of Columbia."

A southern Plains delegation models new outfits from A. Saks and Company on August 2, 1880. Each man received one suit, one valise, one hat, two shirts, one box of collars, one pair of socks, one pair of trousers, a tie, shoes, and underwear at a cost of $23.50 per person. Although the Indians generally took pride in their new suits, one journalist observed that they "looked about as comfortable as bears in moccasins."

Beer and brandy account for a large part of a Chickasaw delegation's bill at the Washington House Hotel in New Jersey, where the group stopped en route to the capital. Although alcohol was illegal in Indian territory, eastern innkeepers had no scruples about plying their guests with drink.

EXPLORING THE SITES OF WASHINGTON

Agents led their Indian guests on whirlwind tours of the District of Columbia, which inevitably included a stop at a military installation to remind them of the whites' superior firepower. Cheyenne and Arapaho delegates who visited the Washington Arsenal in 1851 witnessed a demonstration that proba-

bly included firings of field cannons, giant coastal guns, and the new powerful Colt revolvers. "We are now sure that nothing is impossible to the white people," one chief concluded. "They are next in power to the Great Spirit."

Many groups also visited churches and government buildings and attend-

ed plays and art exhibits where the Indians usually attracted as much attention as the events themselves. After spending three or four weeks in Washington, some delegations made brief visits to Baltimore, Philadelphia, and New York City before returning home. By this time, many of the chieftains had experienced their fill of eastern life. Ten Bears, a Comanche, summed up a common sentiment in 1863 when he complained of having a "big disgust at the noise, confusion, and crowd of the city," and although he appreciated the fine hotels, food, and gifts, he missed his "prairies and dog soup."

A Sioux delegation visiting Washington for talks with President Rutherford B. Hayes in 1877 poses for a group photograph in what was then the Corcoran Art Gallery. The building now houses the Renwick Gallery.

A portrait by George Catlin illustrates the transformation of *The Light*, an Assiniboin who visited Washington, D.C., in 1832. The chieftain is depicted before the visit in traditional garb and with dignified demeanor, and afterward in foppish clothes and with an arrogant attitude that annoyed his fellow tribesmen no end. *The Light's* fantastic stories of city life were particularly vexing, and his description of the multistory Baltimore shot tower proved fatal: An incensed rival took him for a liar and shot him dead.

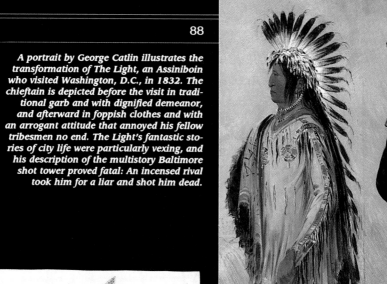

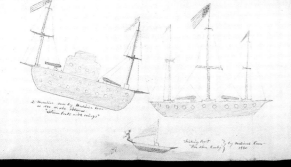

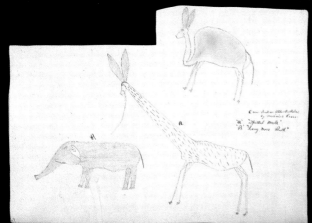

Drawings by Medicine Crow, a member of the Crow delegation to Washington in 1880, recall highlights of his tour. While at the zoo, he encountered several new animals, including an elephant, which he labeled a "long nose bull," and a giraffe, which he called a "spotted mule." He probably saw military ships (above), or "steam boats with wings," on a visit to the Navy Yard.

Piled into two automobiles, a Yankton Sioux delegation poses in front of the U. S. Capitol in 1905. The reviewing stand in the background was probably erected for President Theodore Roosevelt's second inauguration.

The Sioux warrior Moukaushka was so enchanted by one Miss Nelson, a ballerina whom he saw dance at the National Theater in 1837, that he gave her a buffalo robe on the stage as a token of esteem. Other appreciative members of the delegation tossed feathered war bonnets and presented a wolfskin robe to the dancer, who responded by giving each Sioux a feather from her crown of ostrich plumes. The delegates proudly paraded down Pennsylvania Avenue the following day with the plumes tucked into the bands of their new hats.

DOCUMENTING INDIAN CULTURE

By the end of the 19th century, Indians everywhere had been subjugated, and it was no longer necessary to impress them with American might. There was now another motive behind bringing them to Washington: to assemble ethnological details about a people perceived to be a "vanishing race."

In fact, interest in Indian cultures had begun earlier in an unsystematic way. Thomas L. McKenney had established the first museum of Indian artifacts in Washington, D.C., as early as 1818, before the great portrait painters George Catlin and Charles Bird King began their work. But now photographers such as Charles M. Bell could take pictures of Indians in traditional dress. And the Bureau of American Ethnology, founded in 1879, led an effort to record Indian languages and songs.

One unusual endeavor involved making head casts of Indians that served as molds for plaster busts. Luther Standing Bear, a Lakota Sioux student at the Carlisle Indian School who visited the Smithsonian Institution in 1882, was intrigued when curators asked if they could make a bust of his face. His father, however, flatly refused. "My father," Luther wrote, "was quite shocked at the idea of my head being covered with plaster of paris. The idea of my having to breathe through those tubes throughout the process was too much for him!"

An engraving from the September 10, 1881, edition of "Frank Leslie's Illustrated Newspaper" features a visiting delegation, including the Sioux chief White Thunder, sitting for photographs in the studio of Charles M. Bell. The accompanying article describes the Indians as "profuse in thanks when informed that each one would be given copies of his photograph."

Mountain Chief, a Blackfeet Indian, translates a tribal song being played on a phonograph into sign language for ethnologist Frances Densmore in March 1916. Densmore worked tirelessly on a campaign to record aspects of Indian culture, especially music, until her death in 1957.

Nelson Rice, a Pawnee who traveled to Washington in 1887, gave the traditional headdress shown above to the Smithsonian after he had adopted American-style clothing.

Smithsonian curators made a plaster mask of Iron Elk (above), an Oglala Sioux who visited Washington from the Pine Ridge Reservation in the early 1900s. The mask served as a model for the bust at left.

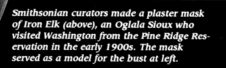

3

CHAMPIONS OF THE APACHE CAUSE

The spring of 1837 was a season of peril for the Apache Indians. Their deep-rooted conflict with the Mexicans had surfaced once again, and the fruits of the struggle promised to be bitter. Incensed by Apache raids on their ranches and towns, officials in Mexico—whose northern territory then embraced most of what is now Arizona and New Mexico—were offering substantial bounties for the scalps of Apache men, women, and children.

A lifetime of struggle is reflected in the furrowed face of the Apache war chief Geronimo, who was confined to an Oklahoma reservation when this photograph was taken in 1905. He spent his last years clinging in vain to the hope that he would be allowed to return to his Arizona homeland.

On April 22, a band of Chiricahua Apaches known as the Mimbres for the river that ran through their mineral-rich homeland were approached at their camp near present-day Silver City, New Mexico, by a trading party that included a man well known to them. He was an Anglo-American adventurer named John James Johnson. The Mimbres's chief, Juan José Compa, had reason to be wary, for his scouts had received word that Mexicans had offered Johnson a special bounty for the chief's scalp.

That officials should put a steep price on Compa's head came as no surprise. Since his father's death at the hands of Mexicans, he had been among their fiercest opponents, rendered all the more dangerous by his knowledge of their ways. Raised in an era of relative peace, he had been educated in Catholic schools and could read Spanish, enabling him to interpret enemy plans intercepted by his scouts.

Still, Compa found it hard to believe that the Mexican offer had been accepted by Johnson, whom he considered his friend. Although the Apache could be devious in battle, they were straightforward in speech, and Compa shared the tendency of his people to trust in the sanctity of oaths. Confronted by the chief outside the Mimbres camp, Johnson assured him that he had no intention of harming him. Compa took Johnson at his word. "You have never deceived me," he told his friend, "and if you give me your word of honor that the report is false, come to my camp with your men and pass the night with us."

Once inside the camp, Johnson exuded goodwill. One of his companions, a man named Gleason, drew Compa away to another part of the camp while Johnson invited the chief's followers to help themselves to some cornmeal piled up in sacks—within which he had concealed a large-bore weapon, loaded with shot. As the Mimbres gathered around, Johnson fired the gun at point-blank range, killing several Apaches and wounding others, who were set upon by Johnson's confederates. Cued by the blast, Gleason drew his own firearm and shot Compa, but the wound was glancing, and the chief managed to wrestle his assailant to the ground. With his knife raised above Gleason's chest, Compa reportedly called for Johnson to intercede and stop the bloodshed, shouting, "I could kill your friend, but don't want to do it!" Johnson responded by taking dead aim at the chief and gunning him down.

Johnson and others in his party made off with the scalps of Compa and perhaps 20 of his followers, for which they later collected a sizable reward. But the attack did not go unavenged. Soon afterward, Apaches massacred 22 members of an American trapping expedition in the area. One innocent white man who barely escaped retribution was trader Benjamin Wilson, who made it safely to Santa Fe and later won renown as the first mayor of Los Angeles. Camped near the massacre site at the time, Wilson heard of Johnson's assault from eyewitnesses and found their account of Compa's desperate appeal to his friend's sense of honor consistent with his own impression of the chief. "I knew him well," he wrote, "and can vouch for the fact that he was a perfect gentleman."

Wilson's tribute would be echoed by other Americans who dealt closely with Apache leaders in years to come. For all their ferocity in battle, these chiefs were men of their word who kept faith with their friends. They refused to abide insults and betrayals, however, and their acts of revenge made them prime targets for white authorities. Mexicans would remain the principal foes of the Apache for some time, but Americans would increasingly be looked on with suspicion as well. After the conclusion of the Mexican War in 1848, those suspicions would give way to outright hostility, as the United States claimed jurisdiction in the region, and American miners, settlers, and soldiers—referred to collectively by the Apache as Pindah, or White Eyes—began to hedge the Apache in. A semi-nomadic people who gained little from working the soil and customarily ranged far to hunt, gather, and raid, the Apache were determined to roam free as always, or to die fighting.

Opposition to the White Eyes emerged among the various Apache tribes—the Mescalero east of the Rio Grande in southeastern New Mexico, the Jicarilla of the upper Rio Grande, and the Western Apache flanking

Geronimo's people, the Chiricahua Apache, led a highly mobile life well suited to the hit-and-run tactics of raiding. As shown in this photograph of a Chiricahua encampment, the Apache sheltered in dome-shaped huts called wickiups, pole-and-brush structures that could be thrown up in less than an hour and abandoned without great loss, features that made them ideal for a people who eluded their enemies by constantly shifting from one place to another.

the Gila and Salt rivers in eastern Arizona. But the hotbed of resistance lay among the Chiricahua of the high New Mexico-Arizona border country. Their proximity to Mexican settlements had conditioned them to conflict, and the steep terrain afforded them shelter from pursuit. From their ranks came not only the defiant Compa but also a cadre of equally formidable chiefs, including Mangas Coloradas, Cochise, Victorio, and Geronimo. Their tactics, which grew bloodier as their people's plight worsened, made them infamous. But to their followers they were heroes, who drew on reserves of tenacity and guile to protect those who relied on them.

The void created among the Mimbres by Compa's death was soon filled by an imposing figure known to the Mexicans as Mangas Coloradas, or

Red Sleeves. Mangas emerged as Compa's successor by the sheer force of his courage and eloquence. For him as for other Apache leaders, authority was earned through words and actions and lasted only so long as the chief commanded the respect of his people. In his case, that respect was not limited to the Mimbres but extended to fellow bands of Eastern Chiricahuas and to other Apaches as well. John R. Bartlett, an American official who dealt frequently with Mangas in the early 1850s, noted that he enjoyed "great influence among the several Apache tribes."

Born in the early 1790s, Mangas was almost 50 years old when he rose to prominence. Yet even at that age, his physical prowess matched the strength of his will. One American who encountered him described him as an "athletic man considerably over six feet in height, with a large broad head covered with a tremendously heavy growth of long hair that reached to his waist. His shoulders were broad and his chest full, and muscular." Like Compa, Mangas aimed most of his fury at Mexicans, deriding them for resorting to scalp hunting, among other stratagems. Asked once why he so despised the Mexicans, he spoke of an incident in which they plied his people with whiskey and then "beat out their brains with clubs." He also cited the attack on Compa by Johnson, whom he described as a trader "sent among us from Chihuahua," thus placing blame for the incident squarely on the Mexicans. "How can we make peace with such people?" he asked.

After Compa's death, Mangas mounted raids of retribution that reduced the nearby copper-mining post of Santa Rita to a ghost town. By 1845 his warriors had wreaked such havoc in the Mexican states of Sonora and Chihuahua that officials there plotted a 1,000-man offensive against him; only a revolution in Mexico kept it from going forward. When war broke out between the United States and Mexico in 1846, the chief met Brigadier General Stephen W. Kearny by a tributary of the Gila River—known to posterity as Mangas Creek—and pledged safe passage through Mimbres country for American forces. He even offered to send some of his own men along with them, an idea Kearny flatly rejected.

At war's end, Mangas hoped to maintain friendly relations with the Americans while continuing raids against the Mexicans. But he soon discovered that the United States meant to establish a secure boundary with Mexico. In 1851 John Bartlett arrived with the U.S. Boundary Commission to survey the country and fix the frontier. Aided by an interpreter, he had several talks with Mangas and urged him to change his ways. "I recommended to him to cultivate the soil," Bartlett wrote, "and raise his own

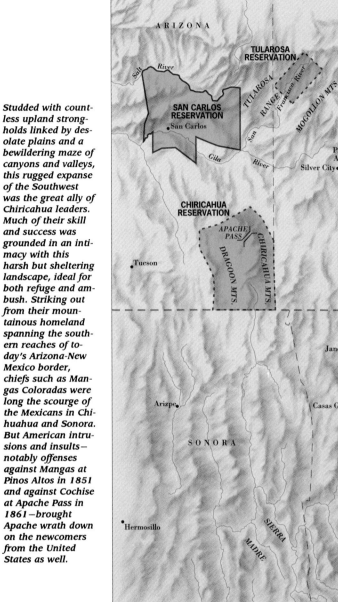

Studded with countless upland strongholds linked by desolate plains and a bewildering maze of canyons and valleys, this rugged expanse of the Southwest was the great ally of Chiricahua leaders. Much of their skill and success was grounded in an intimacy with this harsh but sheltering landscape, ideal for both refuge and ambush. Striking out from their mountainous homeland spanning the southern reaches of today's Arizona-New Mexico border, chiefs such as Mangas Coloradas were long the scourge of the Mexicans in Chihuahua and Sonora. But American intrusions and insults—notably offenses against Mangas at Pinos Altos in 1851 and against Cochise at Apache Pass in 1861—brought Apache wrath down on the newcomers from the United States as well.

corn, mules, horses &c., instead of stealing them from the Mexicans." Mangas responded that he was "too old to begin to raise corn or to cultivate the soil, and that he must leave these things for his young people to do." He complimented the Americans for their bravery, Bartlett added, "but why we should defend the Mexicans, after being at war with them, was to him incomprehensible."

Mangas's diplomatic reply hinted at differences in outlook between the Apache and Americans that would prove irreconcilable. Neither Mangas nor the younger men following him would turn gladly to farming when there were richer rewards to be gleaned by raiding. Farming had never provided much bounty for the Chiricahua, and in any case, it was women's work. Men gained respect by taking up weapons and venturing out to hunt game or to prey on Mexicans whose horses and other live-stock helped nourish the Apache. Inevitably, men had been killed on such raids, and their partners were then obliged to avenge them by mounting expeditions whose sole object was to slay Mexicans or seize them for tor-ture or adoption. The Apache would not lightly abandon such vendettas, for their longing for honor and revenge ran deep and bound one genera-tion to the next. Indeed, efforts by federal officials to thwart the militant traditions of the Apache threatened to earn the Americans a degree of animosity previously reserved for the Mexicans.

Although Bartlett promised that the Boundary Commission and its military escort would be leaving the area as soon as they had finished their work, his men began fixing up abandoned buildings at Santa Rita, feeding Apache fears that outsiders would resettle there. Friction also arose over the issue of Mexican captives, whom Bartlett had been in-structed to return when possible, as required by the recent peace treaty with Mexico. One day, two captive Mexican boys fled from a Mimbres camp, where they had lived for some time, and sought refuge with the commission. Mangas demanded them back. When Bartlett refused, the chief felt betrayed. "You came to our country," he protested. "Your lives, your property, your animals were safe." The Mimbres had made no secret of their Mexican captives. "We concealed nothing," he added. Mangas pointed out that a Mimbres warrior was raising the two boys as his own sons, in keeping with the Apache custom of adopting the women and children they seized. The warrior had grown fond of the boys and wanted them back. Mangas also reminded Bartlett that no one was forcing the Mexicans to return their many young Apache captives, whose fate— usually servitude for the boys and prostitution for the girls—was far worse than that of the Mexican youths.

The issue of captives held special significance for Mangas. Years ear-lier, during a raid, he had seized a young Mexican woman from her vil-lage and made her his wife. The match had met strong opposition from his two Apache wives and their relatives. To settle the matter, Mangas had been forced to fight two of his brothers-in-law in traditional knife duels. He killed both challengers, which left his wives no choice but to accept his decision. His Mexican wife bore him three daughters, whom he later married to prominent warriors of other Apache bands, including Co-chise, leader of the Central Chiricahua. These strategic unions did a great deal to increase Mangas's influence within the region.

Slipped over the right shoulder and passed under the left arm, pendants such as the one shown above were worn by Apache war leaders as a means of providing supernatural protection for themselves and their men in battle. Fashioned from two braided leather thongs embellished with eagle feathers, medicine beans, and bits of stone, the amulet was thought to ward off such hazards as bullets, arrows, and war-club blows.

After several days of tense deliberations, Bartlett and Mangas finally worked out a deal: The commission gave the Apaches blankets and other goods for the youths worth about $250. Yet the incident left Mangas troubled. His concerns were reinforced several weeks later when two Apaches were killed by a Mexican in American territory during a gambling dispute. At the insistence of the Mimbres, the culprit was detained by the Americans, but he was soon released.

Then in the fall of 1851, an incident took place that spurred Mangas into action against the White Eyes. Shortly before that time, prospectors had discovered gold in Pinos Altos, just north of the Santa Rita mines, and eager Americans had flocked to the area. Given to drunken sprees and ever disdainful of the Apache peoples, the newcomers abused the Mimbres without fear of punishment. Mangas may have briefly considered attacking the miners and driving them out, but in the end he sought to lure them away. On a brisk autumn day, he rode into Pinos Altos accompanied by a few of his followers and made a proposal to the prospectors: He would lead them to a secret site in Sonora where the climate was more favorable and the "yellow iron" they desired was even more plentiful.

Mangas's offer may have been genuine, but the prospectors concluded it was a trap. Holding Mangas's men at bay, they seized the chief, tied him to a tree, and whipped him mercilessly. One Mimbres witness later recalled that the miners lashed Mangas "with ox goads until his back was striped with deep cuts." Then they released him, laughing at him as he stumbled off. "He crept away like a wounded animal to let his wounds heal," said the same witness. "Never before had anyone struck him, and there is no humiliation worse than that of a whip."

By shaming the Apache leader in front of his men, the miners put every white person in the region at risk. Once his back had healed, Mangas enlisted the aid of other Chiricahua bands and embarked on a vendetta that claimed scores of lives. No miner's camp, no rancher's hacienda, no stagecoach or wagon train was safe. "The Indians have become bolder and bolder," reported James Calhoun, the ailing governor of the New Mexico Territory. "Such is the daring of the Apache Indians that they openly attack our troops and force them to retreat."

By springtime, Mangas had apparently settled the score to his satisfaction. Notwithstanding his recent humiliation, he still regarded the Mexicans as his principal foes and had no desire to engage in a long war with the United States. So in June of 1852, he and several other chiefs sat down with territorial officials and worked out an accord. The treaty was ratified by the United States Congress and signed by President Franklin Pierce the following spring. Its terms required the Mimbres to recognize the authority of the United States and to refrain from raids into Mexico, but difficulties in translation evidently left Mangas uncertain as to the provisions. Not until the signing ceremony was it made clear to him that his men were to leave the Mexicans alone, and his response was less than enthusiastic. "Are we to be victims of treachery and not be avenged?" he asked. One onlooker concluded that more than signatures on a piece of paper would be needed "to keep these Indians at peace with the people of Old Mexico."

Calhoun's successor, William Lane, tried to bolster the treaty by reaching further agreements with Mangas and other chiefs in the region that were meant to transform the Apache into placid farmers. One such accord bound the Indians to "abandon their wandering and predatory modes of life." A second article required them to "promise hereafter never to resort to the ancient custom of retaliation for any injuries they might suffer." Those were idle expectations, for no Apache chief who enforced such measures would long retain a following. In any case, the import of the articles was probably lost on Mangas and others as interpreters grasped for terms to convey legal concepts foreign to the Apache. What the chiefs did understand was that Lane was promising them regular supplies of food and livestock—provisions their people would greatly need if they were no longer to partake of Mexican booty.

As it turned out, Congress refused to ratify Lane's accords, and few supplies were forthcoming. Facing a long hungry winter, the Mimbres resumed raids on both sides of the border, pilfering provisions worth some $100,000 and claiming several lives in the process. But the U.S. Army was beginning to act decisively to stifle such outbreaks. The troops did not have to defeat Apaches in battle; by driving hostile bands from their camps in winter, they exposed them to cold and famine and left chiefs little choice but to yield. By mid-1855, the army had crushed resistance among the Jicarilla and Mescalero to the east. Heeding the threat, Mangas accepted a new way of life. The government promised his people food and supplies worth $30,000 if they would confine themselves to a reservation along the Mimbres River and concentrate on farming. For the next few years, Mangas and his followers dutifully tended the land and kept peace with the Americans, but they continued their forays into Mexico.

Accommodation with the United States did little to improve the prospects of the Mimbres. Diseases communicated by whites were reducing their population, and the survivors faced constant intimidation from Apache-hating settlers and soldiers. Nor could the Mimbres be sure of retaining the land they farmed. The government had broken many promises to them over the years, and there was talk of moving them farther west onto a reservation near the Gila River.

By 1862 younger Mimbres war leaders were lashing out at the White Eyes, who proved vulnerable now that the demands of the Civil War had stretched their forces thin. Although nearly 70 years old, Mangas decided to join the fray. On July 14, he was at the head of one of several bands that ambushed about 120 infantrymen at Apache Pass, a strategic defile between the Dos Cabezas and Chiricahua mountain ranges in southeastern Arizona. The battle raged for hours. Toward nightfall, Private John Teal, whose horse had been hit by a bullet fired by Mangas, got off a lucky shot that wounded the old chief. The Apaches retreated with their leader to the Mexican town of Janos, where they ordered the local doctor to save the old man's life—or see the town and everyone in it destroyed. Luckily for the people of Janos, Mangas recovered.

Despite his recent conflicts with the White Eyes, Mangas clung to a belief that their word could be trusted. That lingering faith—combined with war-weariness—led to his downfall. In January 1863, he was lured to Pinos Altos by an American offer to talk peace. Once there, he was seized by soldiers flying a white flag and taken to a nearby fort. Brigadier General J. R. West, who believed in using brute force to control the "Indian problem," entrusted Mangas to a guard detail with words that all but sealed his fate. "Men," he reportedly told the guards, "that old murderer

A brilliant moon casts its haunting glow over the Dragoon Mountains in Arizona. This rugged territory was home to the Chiricahua Apache but alien to the soldiers who had to chase them. "They know every water hole and every foot of ground in this vast extent of country," one U.S. Army officer remarked of his resourceful foes.

has got away from every soldier command and has left a trail of blood for 5,000 miles on the old stage line." He then invited the guards to treat the captive Mangas like a killer on the loose: "I want him dead or alive tomorrow morning, do you understand, I want him dead."

They understood. Daniel Conner, a miner laying over at the fort, saw the guards heat their bayonets that evening and apply the steel to Mangas's feet and legs. The chief bore it for a while, then rose up on one elbow and raged at his tormentors. "Thereupon," Conner observed, "the two soldiers, without removing their bayonets from their Minié muskets each fired quickly into the chief, following with two shots each from their Navy six-shooters." The official story was that Mangas had been killed while attempting to overpower the guards and flee.

The following morning, a soldier took Mangas's scalp. His massive skull was later severed and ended up in the hands of a phrenologist, who pronounced it to be of greater size than that of the American statesman Daniel Webster—an empty tribute to a chief whose stature among his people depended on qualities that defied measurement.

The treachery of Mangas's death only deepened the hatred and distrust that many Apaches harbored for Americans. Few resented the deed more than Mangas's son-in-law Cochise. Now about 40 years of age, Cochise was a tall, powerful man who impressed observers as much with his shrewdness as with his strength. Those qualities had earned Cochise the right to succeed his father as chief of the Central Chiricahua, whose territory lay to the southwest of Mimbres country.

Like Mangas, Cochise had been raised to regard Mexicans as the enemy and had tried to be accommodating to Americans—so much so, in fact, that he had agreed in 1858 to safeguard mail coaches passing through his country and to furnish firewood to a new stagecoach station at Apache Pass. The following year, he voluntarily returned stolen livestock to an American mining outfit, telling astonished officials that his men had taken the animals thinking they belonged to Mexicans. But the harmony ended abruptly in 1861 when Cochise discovered that the White Eyes would rather bend him to their will than rely on his word.

In late January of that year, Second Lieutenant George Bascom, an ambitious 25-year-old West Point graduate who had been in Arizona only a few months, reached Apache Pass with 54 infantrymen and requested a meeting with Cochise. The chief went to Bascom's tent, accompanied by several relatives and warriors. After a polite exchange of greetings, Bas-

com abruptly accused Cochise of having seized an 11-year-old boy named Felix during a raid on a nearby ranch, where the boy's Mexican mother lived with the owner, George Ward. The stunned chief said he had no knowledge of the boy—who had evidently been kidnapped by another band of Apaches—but told Bascom he would try to determine the child's whereabouts. Bascom doubted Cochise and ordered his soldiers to seize the chief and his followers, whom he intended to hold as ransom for the boy. Cochise promptly drew a knife from his moccasin, slashed the rear wall of the tent, and escaped into the nearby hills under a flurry of bullets—a getaway celebrated in Apache lore to this day.

Western Apache scouts gather for a portrait in the early 1880s. Unhappy with reservation life and eager for hostilities to end, many Western Apaches joined the U.S. Army and lent their tracking skills to the hunt for Chiricahua chiefs such as Geronimo and Victorio. According to one officer, the scouts could "follow through grass, over sand or rock, up and down the flanks of the steepest ridges, traces so faint that to the keenest-eyed American, they do not appear at all."

Intent on securing the release of the Apaches still being held by Bascom, Cochise gathered an imposing force of warriors and descended on the Apache Pass stagecoach station the next day. Against the advice of Bascom, whose troops were holding the building, the stationmaster there acted on his earlier friendly dealings with Cochise and went out to parley with the chief along with a hosteler and a stagecoach driver named James Wallace. Cochise tried to seize the three as hostages, and firing broke out. The stationmaster and hosteler were shot, and Wallace was carried away by the Apaches. Hours later, Cochise's men ambushed a wagon train west of the station, captured two more Americans, and killed several Mexicans—some of whom were later found tied to the wheels of the wagons, which had been set afire. That night Cochise sent Bascom a note written for him by Wallace. "Treat my people well," it said, "and I will do the same by yours, of whom I have three."

Cochise requested a prisoner exchange, but Bascom refused to trade without the return of young Felix. Cochise may have tried to locate the boy; at one point, a deal between the opponents appeared possible. But then two companies of reinforcements reached Bascom. Fearing attack by a superior force, Cochise and his men slipped away—after first torturing their captives to death. Soldiers later found the mutilated remains. "We came upon three bodies," an infantryman wrote, "one of which, upon examination, I knew to be that of Wallace by the gold filling of some of his teeth, and the other two could be no others than his fellow prisoners. All the bodies were littered with lance holes."

The army promptly retaliated by hanging six Apache hostages from a scrub oak tree. The bodies dangled there for weeks. Among the victims was a brother of Cochise, the chief said later. Enraged by the incident, the once-accommodating Cochise lashed out at Americans at every turn. In the two months following the Bascom affair, he and his avenging warriors were blamed for more than 150 deaths.

By 1862 Cochise had been joined in his campaign against the White Eyes not only by Mangas but also by two other Chiricahua chiefs who were as yet little known to whites but who would subsequently become notorious—Victorio and Geronimo. Under the combined pressure of these Indian leaders, the Americans were forced to abandon the stagecoach line through Apache Pass and redirect coaches along a more northerly route. The Apaches also shut off the vital supply road between the towns of Tucson and Tubac; Tubac was left deserted, and Tucson shrank to an isolated bastion of 200 holdouts.

Mangas's capture and death in 1863 only stiffened Cochise's resolve, and he kept up his relentless attacks on whites for the better part of a decade. He and his fellow chiefs so preoccupied the army that in 1870 General William Tecumseh Sherman wryly observed of the region, "We had one war with Mexico, and we should have another to make her take it back." In time, however, Cochise came to understand, as Mangas had earlier, that however hard his people fought, they could never sweep the White Eyes away. The opposing forces were simply too powerful, and the white settlers too numerous. "We kill ten; a hundred come in their place," Cochise told his warriors. So when word reached him in 1872 that Brigadier General Oliver Otis Howard was traveling from Washington to talk peace, he consented to a meeting.

Howard, who had lost an arm during the Civil War, had been dubbed the "praying general" for his habit of falling to one knee to commune with God at crucial moments. On one occasion before meeting with Cochise, he began praying aloud in the presence of a band of Apaches, who made themselves scarce in fear of this strange "medicine," as one of them put it. Howard later tried to convince the band's leader of his peaceful intentions. "Could I not come into your lodges at any time—even

TOKENS OF DIPLOMACY

In an effort to win favor among the Indians, the rival European nations on North American soil—Spain, Great Britain, and France—initiated the practice of bestowing important-seeming medals upon tribal chieftains. The fledgling United States continued the custom, creating its first medal during George Washington's administration. Presented at treaty signings and on other special occasions, these medals featured the likeness of the incumbent president on one side and a symbol of friendship and goodwill on the other.

In the latter half of the 19th century, as the tribes were gradually subdued and resettled on reservations, officials began to change the motif of the medals as part of the effort to persuade Indians to abandon their warring and hunting traditions and adopt American ways. Peace pipes and clasped hands gave way to scenes of Indians engaged in such tranquil agrarian pursuits as woodchopping and plowing. The medals that had once symbolized the diplomatic ties between sovereign nations became little more than trinkets used to reward individual Indians for serving the government's interests. Enthusiasm for awards such as these eventually waned, and it was during the administration of Benjamin Harrison, 1889–1893, that the last of the Indian medals was struck.

Iron Bear, a Yankton Sioux leader, proudly wears his Andrew Johnson medal.

In the government's eyes, the Indian farmer on the Benjamin Harrison medal, having adopted a "civilized occupation," symbolized progress. The medal was presented to an Arapaho leader named Paul Boynton.

Handcrafted from silver, the George Washington issue was the first peace medallion produced by the United States government.

The hollow Thomas Jefferson medal drew complaints from those chiefs who had become accustomed to the heft of the solid British and George Washington issues.

Great Britain rewarded its Indian allies by the presentation of a solid silver medal featuring the bust of King George III.

when you are on the warpath?'' he inquired innocently. To which the chief responded, ''Not unless you want to get killed.''

After this discomfiting lesson in diplomacy, Howard proceeded to his conference with Cochise under the escort of two Chiricahua warriors and the only white man Cochise ever completely trusted—Thomas Jeffords. A former stagecoach driver and superintendent of U.S. mails who had once been wounded in an Apache ambush, Jeffords had astonished Cochise several years earlier by walking alone and unarmed into his camp to negotiate a truce. Besides being impressed with Jeffords's bravery, Cochise admired him for his sincerity. Jeffords returned the compliment, remarking of the chief, ''He was a man who scorned a liar.'' The two became enduring friends. Cochise made a pledge to Jeffords that no Chiricahua would ever harm him, and none ever did.

Jeffords led Howard to an imposing canyon in the foothills of the Dragoon Mountains where they camped for the night, anxiously awaiting word from Cochise. The chief and his party arrived the following morning. Cochise greeted Howard with a pleasant, *''Buenos días, señor.''* The two leaders then sat down to talk. Howard explained that President Ulysses S. Grant had sent him to make peace with the Chiricahua. ''Nobody wants peace more than I do,'' Cochise replied. Howard then outlined the government's offer to resettle Cochise and his people on a reservation just west of the Rio Grande near the town of Cañada Alamosa (present-day Monticello, New Mexico) some 150 miles to the northeast. The area would provide ample water and good pasture for cattle, he noted. Cochise knew the place, and considered the idea for a while. Then he countered with his own proposal. ''Rather than not have peace,'' he said, ''I will go there and take such of my people as I can, but that move will break up my tribe.'' Why should his people not remain around Apache Pass, he asked. ''Give me that and I will protect all the roads. I will see that nobody's property is taken.''

The talks continued for 11 days as Cochise awaited the arrival of other Chiricahua leaders, whom he had to consult before making any agreement with the government. As time passed, Howard listened to Cochise with growing appreciation. ''We were once a large people covering these mountains,'' Cochise told him. ''We lived well; we were at peace.'' But Bascom made an enemy of him, he added, by killing his brother and others dear to him and denying them the proper burial rites: ''Their bodies were hung up and kept there till they were skeletons.'' Cochise went on to explain his decision to make peace: ''I have killed 10 white men for every Indian slain, but I know that the whites are many and the Indians are few." Cochise then pleaded again for his homeland. "Why shut me up on a reservation?" he asked. "We will make peace; we will keep it faithfully. But let us go around free as Americans do."

The poignant words of Cochise had a disarming effect on the general. In the end, the chief won his point. "I was forced to abandon the Alamosa scheme," Howard reported to his superiors, "and to give them, as Cochise had suggested, a reservation embracing a part of the Chiricahua Mountains and of the valley adjoining on the west." Furthermore, at Cochise's request, Howard agreed to appoint Jeffords as the government's agent to the Central Chiricahua.

Sadly, however, the treaty worked out between the general and the chief did not last, in part because other government officials mistakenly assumed that Cochise, a regional chief, had authority over all of the diverse Apache bands that were operating in the area. By 1874, citing continued Apache raids and wrongly blaming them on Cochise, the United States Bureau of Indian Affairs declared the Chiricahua reservation project a failure and instructed Cochise to move his people to Cañada Alamosa. Cochise told officials that his Chiricahua would not go. "The government has not enough troops to move them," he said, "as they would rather die here than move there."

His words proved true. Within a few years, hundreds of Chiricahuas would run off to live as renegades rather than relocate. Cochise, however, did not live to witness the scattering of his people. In May of 1874, his health failed him. Levi Dudley, superintendent of Indian affairs for New Mexico, noted that even whites in the region feared his approaching death. "To hear fear expressed that the greatest and most warlike Apache might die sounded strange enough," he remarked, "but when I ascertained that the great chief retained in peace the wonderful power and influence he had exercised in war, and that he regarded his promises made to General Howard sacred and not to be violated upon any pretext whatever, I knew that it would be a calamity to the frontier to lose him from the ranks of living men."

In June, Cochise named his son Taza as his successor and made him promise to keep peace. Then he met one last time with Jeffords.

"Brother, do you think you will ever see me alive again?" he asked.

"No," Jeffords replied. "I think by tomorrow night you will be dead."

"Yes, I think so—about 10 o'clock tomorrow morning. Do you think we will ever meet again?"

"I don't know," Jeffords answered. "What is your opinion?"

"I believe good friends will meet somewhere," responded the Indian.

Cochise died at the hour he had appointed. His followers painted his body yellow, black, and vermilion, in accordance with Chiricahua custom, and sealed it in an unmarked cave.

Cochise was not the only Apache chief who opposed the forced movement of his people onto a reservation far from their homeland. The Mimbres leader Victorio, who took up where Mangas left off, fought equally hard to keep his followers from being exiled from their ancestral ground. A master of feints and dodges who seemed to anticipate his enemy's every move, Victorio foiled his American adversaries so thoroughly in the late 1870s that one officer called him the "greatest Indian general who had ever appeared on the American continent."

Like a number of his fellow Apaches—who picked up elements of Mexican culture along with the captives and booty they seized—Victorio acquired a Spanish name, meaning "the triumphant one," a tribute to his prowess as a war leader. Im-

Detained by the U.S. Army, Victorio, chief of New Mexico's Mimbres Apache, reportedly scuffled with two soldiers and had to be physically restrained for this photograph. The picture was taken sometime after 1877, the year his people were driven from their Warm Springs homeland and forced to live on the San Carlos Reservation in Arizona.

pressed by his cleverness, Mexicans would claim Victorio as one of their own, citing unverified reports that he had been seized and adopted by the Mimbres as a boy. The Apache, for their part, gave no credence to such tales. For all his cunning on the warpath, Victorio was unusually scrupulous when he had enemies at his mercy. The men his band captured were often killed but rarely tortured—as such prisoners generally were by the followers of other Apache chiefs. Although the plunder he acquired through raids could have afforded him many wives, he chose to have only one and provided generously for their five children and other kin.

Victorio's elusiveness on the warpath was all the more remarkable for the fact that he and his warriors seldom went far without their women and youngsters. In the old days, before the bounty hunters and soldiers arrived, war parties had often left their families behind for weeks on end, confident that few outsiders had the savvy or temerity to trespass on their domain. But now many White Eyes were wise to Apache ways and could track down encampments in the most remote settings. If the soldiers were ignorant of the terrain, they could call on the services of Apache scouts from tribes that had been pacified for years and whose people felt few qualms about opposing the Mimbres or other resistant groups.

Although Victorio figured in the Chiricahua uprising of the early 1860s, he was best known for his long struggle against federal relocation policies that intensified about the time of Cochise's death. By 1870 Victorio had willingly taken his band of Mimbres to live on the Cañada Alamosa Reservation, also known as the Warm Springs Agency. Although that place was alien to Cochise's people, it was dear to the Mimbres. White settlers wanted the arable land there, but feared Apache raids and urged the government to move the Mimbres elsewhere. Heeding those appeals, officials in 1872 ordered Victorio to move his people 60 miles to the northwest to another reservation in the Tularosa Valley, a site that the Apache despised. Cochise had roundly condemned Tularosa as a home to "bad spirits" and a place where flies "eat out the eyes of horses." After languishing there awhile, the Mimbres were allowed to return to Warm Springs in 1874, only to learn that they were soon to be consigned to a wasteland worse than Tularosa.

That same year, the Bureau of Indian Affairs adopted a new policy of "concentration." All the various Apache bands would be placed together under military supervision on the San Carlos Reservation, a hot, barren tract of some 5,000 square miles in southeastern Arizona. Victorio reluctantly agreed to go to San Carlos with his people—after first stashing away their best weapons in the event conditions there proved intolerable. Overcrowded, poorly supplied with rations, and fraught with administrative corruption, San Carlos was a miserable place. "Hell's Forty Acres," one officer assigned to supervise Apaches there dubbed the place.

By the late summer of 1877, Victorio had seen enough of it. On September 2, shortly before dawn, he and another Mimbres chief called Loco broke out of San Carlos with about 300 of their followers and headed for New Mexico, stealing horses and other stock as they went. Troops followed in pursuit, and several sharp skirmishes ensued that claimed the lives of about a dozen white ranchers and soldiers and 50 Mimbres warriors—a toll Victorio could ill afford. Soon he surrendered to the army at a fort on the border of Navajo country, with assurances from the presiding officer that he would try to persuade Washington to allow the Mimbres to settle at Warm Springs permanently if they would agree in turn to renounce hostilities. Victorio and his people lived amicably at Warm Springs for the next year, winning unaccustomed praise from local white settlers. Ignoring this earnest show of cooperation, Washington elected to send the Mimbres back to San Carlos. The bitter Victorio vanished once again into the mountains with some 100 warriors. With winter coming on, they had to leave behind their women and children, who were soon conducted to San Carlos by the army.

During the months ahead, Victorio's men faced terrible hardship, and he offered more than once to cooperate with authorities if they would relent and reunite his people at Warm Springs. He disliked the life of a renegade, he told the army. But events soon conspired to thrust him back into that role with a vengeance. In the summer of 1879, a grand jury in Silver City issued indictments against Victorio for horse theft and murder—deeds for which another Apache chief may in fact have been responsible. The charges strained Victorio's forbearance to the breaking point. He never saw the indictment, but he knew that there was a "paper" out against him. In his experience, the Americans took what they committed to paper seriously when it came to punishing Apaches, although they often ignored what they had written down when their own treatment of the Indians was in question.

A short time later, while Victorio was conferring with officials at the Tularosa Reservation, the district attorney and judge who had presided over the Silver City indictments showed up there. The district attorney, Albert Fountain, said afterward that he and the judge were just passing through with friends to hunt and fish. When their presence became known to Victorio, however, he could only assume that they meant to bring him in. Concluding that authorities had conspired against him, he rode off with his followers in a fury and triggered one of the bloodiest episodes in the history of the Apache conflicts.

Renouncing all hope of ever coming to terms with the White Eyes, Victorio and his warriors clashed with soldiers and civilians alike. They made a point of stealing or killing livestock, not just for their own use but to deny sustenance and mobility to the enemy. Victorio would lure pursuing troops into canyons and defiles where his men had the advantage

Geronimo's rifle leans against the ruins of the Warm Springs Agency in New Mexico, where the warrior chief sought refuge among Victorio's people. An Indian agent and his Apache police arrested Geronimo at Warm Springs in 1877; he was later released, but the rifle was kept as a souvenir.

Geronimo stands defiantly with his current rifle, a powerful Springfield, after surrendering to General George Crook in March 1886. For close-quarters fighting, he could turn to his Colt .45 (below) and a factory-made knife (opposite), weapons he kept in a holster and sheath attached to a silver-studded belt (top).

of the terrain and could pick off cavalrymen and their mounts with virtual impunity. One officer whose men were ambushed near the head of Animas Creek lost a civilian volunteer, two Navajo scouts, five soldiers, and 32 horses before darkness descended and enabled his force to withdraw. "My cavalry will be principally dismounted," he reported ruefully. Indian agent Samuel Russell lamented that the efforts of such units amounted to the "frequent *trailing* of these Indians, without (so far as I know) ever catching any."

After a year on the run, Victorio's band was credited with having taken hundreds of lives. How many of his own men were lost in the process is unknown, but his force reportedly grew larger over the months, reaching a peak of perhaps 300 warriors as restive members of other tribes joined him. A number of women and children came along with the fighting men. Among the Apache youngsters was James Kaywaykla, who later recalled the harrowing odyssey: "For weeks we fled from one range to another, crossing the open plains at night, with a strong advance guard preceding the women and children, and warriors bringing up the rear. Children rode tied to horses and to adults."

Some of the elderly were left at hideaways along with newborns and their mothers, he added, "but the great majority kept on, with little food, with no fires, and often with terrible weakness and fatigue, but without complaint." To Victorio's followers, this journey was not a heedless rampage—as some whites perceived it—but a search for sanctuary.

In the end, it was Victorio's old enemies the Mexicans who brought him down. Near sundown on October 14, 1880, after the chief had led his people south across the border, the veteran Apache fighter Joaquin Terrazas caught Victorio by surprise and forced him and many members of his party up the southernmost promontory of the Tres Castillos, three isolated Mexican peaks located about halfway between El Paso and the city of Chihuahua. That night, as the fighting ebbed, the stranded Apaches began singing their death songs. About dawn the following day, Terrazas moved in for the kill. Victorio's people fought furiously, but they quickly ran out of ammunition. Seventy-eight Apaches, including 18 women and children, died in the massacre, while Terrazas lost only three soldiers.

Victorio was among the casualties. He was reportedly shot by an Indian scout accompanying the Mexicans, a man named Mauricio. The Mexican government awarded the scout a nickel-plated rifle and a bounty of 3,000 American dollars for firing the fatal bullet. Yet Apaches who later recovered the victims' bodies told another story. They said Victorio—who dreaded confinement more than death—had stabbed himself with his knife rather than be captured by his enemies.

After hiding out for several months, some of Victorio's surviving followers linked up with a small band that was led by the war chief Geronimo. Like Victorio, he had recently fled the San Carlos Reservation and was on the run from the U.S. Army. Before troops cornered him for good, he would come to epitomize the spirit of Apache resistance.

Unlike many other Chiricahuas, who grew up in an atmosphere of conflict, Geronimo had been blessed with a peaceful childhood. Born in the late 1820s amid the remote Mogollon Mountains, where Indians in ancient times had sought shelter in cliff dwellings, he was given the unassuming name of Goyahkla, meaning One Who Yawns. His people were the Bedonkohe, a branch of the Eastern Chiricahua, and for some time they remained isolated. "During my minority," he later recalled, "we had never seen a missionary or a priest. We had never seen a white man. Thus, quietly lived the Bedonkohe Apaches."

When Goyahkla was nearly an adult, his father became ill and died, and he went with his mother to live with relatives among the Nednhi, or Southern Chiricahua, in Chihuahua. The Nednhi were in conflict with the Mexicans, and Goyahkla underwent the rigorous initiation required of all would-be Apache warriors, embarking on four raids as an apprentice to assist his elders before being accepted as a full-fledged fighting man. By the age of 17, he had entered the council of warriors and earned the right to marry. He chose a slender Nednhi girl named Alope for his wife. To her father he paid a handsome dowry of ponies—acquired, no doubt, during forays against the Mexicans. Shortly after his marriage, he returned with his wife and his mother to the Bedonkohe, who had at that time united with other bands of Chiricahuas under the leadership of Mangas.

Those were treacherous times for Goyahkla and his fellow tribesmen. Nevertheless, he managed to raise three children with Alope and keep them safe—until one summer in the 1850s, when they followed Mangas south across the border into Chihuahua. There they traded and accepted goods from Mexican officials who were offering the handouts in the hope of appeasing Apache raiders. Even as Chihuahuans were making concessions, however, Sonorans were out hunting for Apaches. One day, while Goyahkla and other warriors were away from their camp near Janos, Sonoran troops attacked and overpowered the men who had been left behind and massacred scores of people— among them Goyahkla's mother, wife, and children. Fearing a second assault, the stunned Apaches fled, and Goyahkla did not even have the opportunity to recover the bodies of his relatives. "I did not pray," he remarked later, "nor did I resolve to do anything in particular, for I had no purpose left. I finally followed the tribe silently, keeping just within hearing distance of the soft noise of the feet of the retreating Apaches." A short time afterward, while he grieved alone for his family, he had a vision whose power remained with him for the rest of his days. He heard a voice call his name four times—a sacred number. Then the voice said:

Made from buckskin and adorned with eagle feathers and ribbons, the ceremonial headdress shown at left belonged to Geronimo, who donned it for the photograph above. The spiritual powers he possessed as an eminent shaman served him well in his role as war leader; according to his followers, supernatural visions revealed the whereabouts of his enemies, making it possible for him to elude and frustrate them.

"No gun can ever kill you. I will take the bullets from the guns of the Mexicans, so they will have nothing but powder."

Confident that spirits were watching over him, Goyahkla awaited his chance to avenge the deaths of his loved ones. The opportunity came the following summer when he descended with his fellow warriors on the Sonoran town of Arizpe, where troops were stationed. On the third and final day of fighting, Goyahkla—as yet untested as a war leader—was chosen to direct the attack. Ranging up front, he mounted charge after charge. Each time he did so, it was said, the Mexicans screamed, "Geronimo!"—a plea to Saint Jerome, their patron saint—a name the Apache warrior wore with pride thereafter.

The clash at Arizpe brought Geronimo not only revenge but also increased authority among his people. After the murder of Mangas, he sometimes rode with Cochise and Victorio on their raids against Americans, but more often he struck off on his own with his small but loyal band of followers. Confined more than once to the San Carlos Reservation, he broke out again shortly after Victorio was killed and joined up with remnants of Victorio's band in the Sierra Madre. Such was his opposition to the White Eyes by this time that he was prepared to attack any Indian who aided them. In April of 1882, he staged an audacious raid on San Carlos, evading federal troops and compelling Apaches there to leave the compound and join his renegades. "No one is to be left in camp," he reportedly told his warriors. "Shoot down anyone who refuses to go with us." Among those killed by Geronimo's men was the chief of the Indian police who helped patrol the reservation. After the raid, hundreds of Apaches left San Carlos with Geronimo and headed south for the rugged border country, where they clashed with American forces as well as Mexican troops.

As the pressure mounted on Geronimo and his warriors, he gained a reputation for being able to see things that were hidden to others. In May of 1883, he left his main camp in the Sierra Madre and went off on a raid with part of his band, including his cousin and confederate Jason Betzinez. After they had been on the trail for a few days, Betzinez recalled afterward, Geronimo startled his followers by announcing to them around the fire, "Men, our people whom we left at our base camp are now in the hands of U.S. troops." The men hurried back with their leader and found to their dismay that what he said was true. With most of his warriors and their families in enemy hands, he had little choice but to surrender to Brigadier General George Crook, who had crossed the border with permission from Mexican officials and surrounded the camp with the help of Apache scouts.

Crook conducted 52 men and 273 women and children back to San Carlos, but allowed the chief the face-saving option of reporting to that hated place under his own authority, confident that he would sooner die than abandon his people to their fate. The general was correct. Nine months later, Geronimo and a few confederates arrived at San Carlos, trailing 350 head of cattle. Geronimo regarded this Mexican livestock as legitimate spoils and intended to distribute the bounty to his people, but the army confiscated the herd.

Although General Crook sought to make San Carlos a more tolerable place for the Apaches, Geronimo remained defiant. Flouting reservation rules that forbade many Apache customs—particularly the brewing of tiswin, a traditional Apache beer made from fermented corn—Geronimo and a dozen other leaders staged a drinking spree, then openly challenged the authorities. "We all drank tiswin last night," one of the rebels shouted at the presiding lieutenant, "What are you going to do about it? Are you going to put us all in jail?" The officer responded that he would report the matter to the distant Crook. As the days passed, an edgy Geronimo began to credit rumors that Crook was gathering a force to arrest and execute him. In May of 1885, he bolted from San Carlos for the last time, heading south toward Mexico with four other chiefs, about 40 warriors, and perhaps 100 women and children. Two of the chiefs evidently quarreled with Geronimo and split off with their followers, fostering the impression that Apaches were scouring the area in a campaign of terror. Newspapers trumpeted the warning, "The Apaches Are Out!" and fear gripped the occupants of the remote ranches, mines, and way stations along the Mexican border.

The danger was real: Dozens of whites, including many civilians, perished in the days ahead as the Apaches pillaged for horses and supplies. Geronimo received full blame, although in reality much of the mayhem

After yielding to federal troops for good, Geronimo (front row, center) and his followers rest on a railroad embankment in Texas during their 1886 journey to a Florida prison. To Geronimo's right is Naiche, son of Cochise and chief of the Central Chiricahua. All told, some 500 Chiricahuas were sent to Florida from Arizona reservations; among them were scouts who had helped track down Geronimo and other tribal leaders.

was the work of one of the breakaway chiefs, who rejoined Geronimo south of the border in June. Mexico proved to be no haven for the renegades, however. General Crook dispatched two columns of soldiers and Apache scouts to track them down. In January 1886, Crook's troops seized Geronimo's mountain hideout and claimed all the ponies and possessions, although the Apaches themselves escaped. Demoralized and tired of being hunted, Geronimo's followers pressed him to settle with Crook. Reluctantly, Geronimo met with the general. "Do with me what you please," he told Crook. "Once I moved about like the wind. Now I surrender to you and that is all."

Nevertheless, the old warrior had one last surprise in store for the White Eyes. Later that night, after receiving erroneous reports that the army planned to hang him and his followers, Geronimo renounced surrender and fled into the drizzling rain accompanied by a mere 20 warriors and perhaps as many women and children.

A few weeks later, the beleaguered General Crook, under fire for letting Geronimo slip away, angrily resigned his command. His successor, the ambitious Brigadier General Nelson A. Miles, implemented a Washington order to exile all of the Chiricahua peoples, including those who had remained peacefully at San Carlos, to a Florida reservation. He also instigated a huge manhunt for Geronimo, mobilizing 5,000 troops—one-fourth of the entire U.S. Army—against the lone chief and his few followers. Yet the small size of Geronimo's band helped him to elude pursuit and continue raiding. "We were reckless of our lives because we felt that every man's hand was against us," Geronimo later explained. "If we returned to the reservation, we would be put in prison and killed; if we stayed in Mexico, they would continue to send soldiers to fight us; so we gave no quarter to anyone and asked no favors."

Ultimately,. the Apache scouts who had done so much to frustrate Geronimo in the preceding years helped bring him to bay. In late August 1886, General Miles decided to attempt to talk his elusive foe into surrendering. He dispatched an emissary whom Geronimo trusted, a courageous young lieutenant named Charles Gatewood, to locate the chief at his camp. To assist him in his mission, the envoy was accompanied by two scouts who knew the country well, including a Nednhi Apache by the name of Martine. One of Geronimo's followers later described the fateful moment when the scouts approached the band's mountain hideout. "The

Geronimo (left), Naiche (right), and Mangus (center), son of the warrior Mangas Coloradas, sit idly among obsolete cannons at Fort Pickens in Pensacola, Florida. Even though the government promised Geronimo that he and his men would live with their families, the women and children were initially confined at Fort Marion in Saint Augustine, approximately 400 miles away.

Geronimo and his family display melons gathered from their patch at Fort Sill, Oklahoma, where the Chiricahua were relocated in 1894 after a move from Alabama. The majority of the Chiricahua men, hunters by tradition, resisted government efforts to transform them into farmers; Geronimo, however, flourished in the role.

two scouts kept on climbing," he recalled. "Martine was carrying a stick with a white rag on it. I could see their faces and told Geronimo who they were." The chief responded with characteristic scorn for Apaches who abetted the White Eyes. "It does not matter who they are," he said. "If they come closer they are to be shot."

But no Apache leader—not even Geronimo—could compel his men to obey him against their better judgment. As one of his followers said to him defiantly, the scouts were their brothers and brave men and deserved a hearing. Grudgingly, Geronimo gave in and spoke with the scouts. They told him that many of his friends and kin had already been sent to Florida. They reminded him that everything was against him: "Mexicans, White Eyes, and even the beasts"—all were his foes. They persuaded him finally to meet with Gatewood and ponder his words.

Within days, Geronimo had yielded to General Miles and was bound for Florida, where he would be imprisoned for two years before rejoining his kin on the reservation there. Credit for snaring the last great Apache renegade would go to Miles and his men. But it was Geronimo's own people who induced him to bow to the inevitable. ❖

CHIEF JOSEPH'S WAR

Throughout the summer of 1877, newspaper and magazine readers across the United States were riveted by accounts of an extraordinary David-and-Goliath saga that was unfolding in the Northwest wilderness. Some 750 Nez Percé men, women, and children who had been forced out of their homeland were persistently beating back vastly superior United States Army forces pursuing them in a desperate 1,700-mile odyssey. The astonishing success of the Indians—whose battle force consisted of fewer than 200 warriors—was attributed to the tactical genius of the Nez Percé leader, Chief Joseph, the man who came to be known as the Indian Napoleon.

Chief Joseph, in fact, while a genuinely heroic figure, was not a Napoleonic leader at all. This popular notion of his role was symptomatic of how whites misunderstood the Nez Percé and their egalitarian leadership structure. A tribe numbering about 3,600, recognized as among North America's preeminent horse breeders, they had long lived in small settlements scattered across some 12,000 square miles of lush grazing land and steep mountains covering much of present-day northern Idaho and stretching into what is now southeastern Washington State and northeastern Oregon. Villages in close proximity to one another were loosely organized into autonomous bands, each directed in peacetime by a civil chief and in battle by a war leader. There was no head chief, and leaders were empowered to speak only for their own bands, never for the tribe as a whole.

Friendly to whites from the first, many of the Nez Percé were receptive to the teachings of Christian missionaries. One of the first converts was Old Joseph, chief of a band that occupied Oregon's beautiful Wallowa Valley. In 1855 Old Joseph joined all 55 other Nez Percé chiefs in signing a treaty that ceded a small portion of their tribal range to the U.S. government. In return, they were to receive $200,000 and unrestricted rights to the remainder of their ancestral domain.

The treaty failed to achieve the peace the tribal leaders so earnestly desired. In 1860 gold was discovered in Nez Percé territory. Miners poured in, followed by ranchers and farmers. By mid-1862, more than 18,000 whites had settled illegally on the reservation, and many were pressing the government to move the Indians elsewhere. Congress authorized funds to purchase additional land.

The ensuing negotiations permanently split the tribe into two bitterly opposed factions. The government proposed to shrink the reservation to one-tenth its size—1,200 square miles in Idaho. The Indians who already lived there were largely willing to sign. But most of those whose villages lay outside the new boundaries rejected the proposal and angrily walked out of the conference. Among the dissenters was Old Joseph, who tore up his copy of the 1855 agreement and the Bible he had carried with him since his baptism, 24 years earlier.

Since the traditional structure of Nez Percé society did not provide for a head chief, government negotiators simply conferred that honor on a man of their own choosing. He was an obliging English speaker called Lawyer, who had no standing as a chief among his own people. Lawyer signed the new treaty and ignited more than a decade of incendiary dispute.

The U.S. General Land Office, assured by treaty commissioners that they had obtained legal title to the land, surveyed the territory and declared it open for settlement. The nontreaty chiefs, insisting that Lawyer had no right to deal away their homeland in his "Thief Treaty," as they called it, remained defiant. In August 1871, as Old Joseph lay dying, he summoned his son and successor, 31-year-old Hin-mah-too-yah-lat-keht (Thunder Traveling to Loftier Mountain Heights), also known as Young Joseph. "You must stop your ears whenever you are asked to sign a treaty selling your home," commanded the old chief. "Never forget my dying words. This country holds your father's body. Never sell the bones of your father and mother."

A buffalo-hide gun case was found abandoned on the banks of the Clearwater River after the Nez Percé clashed with federal troops there in July 1877.

C A N A D A

Scale of Miles

0   50   100   150   200

BEAR'S PAW

Missouri River

ROUTE OF
COL. MILES

WASHINGTON
TERRITORY

Columbia River

BITTERROOT

FT. MISSOULA

M O N T A N A   T E R R I T O R Y

Yellowstone River

FT. KEOGH

Snake

River

NEZ PERCÉ
RESERVATION

FT. FIZZLE

LOLO PASS

Missouri River

Musselshell River

ROUTE OF COL. STURGIS
AND 7TH CAVALRY

FT.
WALLA
WALLA

FT. LAPWAI

WEIPPE PRAIRIE

Bitterroot R.

Stevensville

CLEARWATER

LOOKING
GLASS'S CAMP

GIBBON'S
MARCH

DUG BAR

CAMAS PRAIRIE

CANYON
CREEK

WHITE
BIRD

BIG HOLE

*Wallowa
Lake*

Salmon

River

MTS.

ABSAROKA MTS.

Clark's Fork

WALLOWA MTS.

YELLOWSTONE
NATIONAL PARK

Shoshone River

OREGON

W Y O M I N G   T E R R I T O R Y

I D A H O   T E R R I T O R Y

BOUNDARY OF NEZ PERCÉ HOMELAND

The treaty of 1855 set aside most of the Nez Percé's original homeland, including the 3,145-square-mile Wallowa Valley in northeastern Oregon, as a reservation (outlined in green). The 1863 agreement reduced their holdings to 1,200 square miles (shaded area) in Idaho. Forced out of the Wallowa in May 1877, Chief Joseph's band crossed the Snake River into Idaho to meet the other exiled bands near Tolo Lake. There they began their 1,700-mile flight for freedom, shown on the map in red.

Christian Chiefs Jason (near left) and Timothy, who signed the 1863 treaty, belonged to a tribal faction that sought to assimilate their people into white society.

FAREWELL TO THE WALLOWA

I have heard about a bargain, a trade betwee concerning their land; but I belong to the land o

WALLOWA LAKE IN OREGON

A tall, powerfully built man whose handsome features expressed gentleness and a keen intelligence, Chief Joseph was driven all his life by love for his "beautiful valley of winding waters."

Young Chief Joseph was a committed pacifist. Determined to achieve justice for his people peacefully, he met repeatedly with white officials, impressing them with his dignity and eloquence. Many were convinced his cause was just. "In my opinion," reported one investigator in 1875, "the nontreaty Nez Percé cannot in law be regarded as bound by the treaty of 1863."

The government conceded that the nontreaty chiefs were entitled to compensation for their land but insisted that they sell. The negotiations culminated in a May 1877 council at Fort Lapwai. There the nontreaty bands led by Joseph and his eastern neighbors, Chiefs White Bird and Toohoolhoolzote, met with Brigadier General Oliver Otis Howard, military commander of the territory. The talks ended with an angry exchange between Howard and the fiercely uncompromising Toohoolhoolzote, whom the Indians had selected as their spokesman. Infuriated by the old warrior's insistence that he would never sell his "Mother Earth," Howard issued a blunt ultimatum: Move to the reservation in 30 days, or the army would resort to force. Recognizing that resistance would bring terrible suffering to their people, the chiefs yielded. Joseph returned to the Wallowa and persuaded his followers to comply. Sorrowfully, they made their way east to the Snake River at Dug Bar Crossing.

ome of these Indians and the white men
f which I came. The earth is my mother.

- TOOHOOLHOOLZOTE

THE SNAKE RIVER AT DUG BAR CROSSING

These young men have come from Whi belonging to a white settler they kille

Yellow Buffalo Bull, a warrior of the White
Bird band, took part in the second spate
of reprisals against whites that helped seal
the fate of the nontreaty Nez Percé.

Bird country, bringing horses with them. Horses
Killed yesterday sun! It will have to be war!

— TWO MOONS

After fording the torrential Snake, Joseph's people headed to Tepahlewam (Split Rocks), the ancient counciling site on the Camas Prairie beside Tolo Lake. There on June 2, only 12 days before they had to be on the reservation, they camped with bands of other nontreaty Nez Percé.

Joseph and his younger brother Ollokot, the war leader of the Wallowa band, left camp to butcher some cattle they had been forced to leave behind. While they were gone, disaster struck.

On June 13, a young member of White Bird's band named Wahlitits, along with two friends, rode back to his Salmon River homeland to avenge the death of his father, killed two years earlier by a white man. The young men never found the murderer, but they did kill four whites who were known to have mistreated Indians in the past.

The triumphant return of one of the youths astride a stolen roan stallion threw the camp into an uproar. Inspired by the deed, a war party of 17 headed up the Salmon to join the other young men and settle more old scores—killing or wounding a dozen more whites over the next two days.

Many in the camp reacted with horror, realizing that Howard would not let the killings go unanswered. To shield their people from white wrath, White Bird and Toohoolhoolzote immediately broke camp and fled. Joseph and Ollokot, who returned on June 15, hoped to persuade Howard not to punish all the Nez Percé for the intemperate actions of a few. But that night shots were fired into their tipis, convincing Joseph that white passions were running too high for a reasoned solution. He and his followers packed up and set off to join the others.

THE CAMAS PRAIRIE NEAR TOLO LAKE

INITIAL VICTORY FOR THE NEZ PERCÉ

So stripped for war, I mounted my horse and rode swiftly along with the strung-out riders, some of them carrying bows and arrows only. Soon the soldiers started firing.

— ROARING EAGLE

An imposing figure celebrated for his exuberance and daring, Joseph's beloved younger brother Ollokot was the chief tactician of the Wallowa band.

THE BATTLEFIELD AT WHITE BIRD CREEK

As the fugitive bands turned south into the protective hills along White Bird Canyon, they were pursued by two companies of soldiers under Captain David Perry. On June 17, in one final attempt to avert war, six Nez Percés rode out under a white flag to parley. Perry's lead scout, a civilian volunteer, fired impulsively on the Indians, ending the last hopes for peace.

In the battle that followed, a Nez Percé force of no more than 70 warriors, armed with bows and arrows and antiquated guns, handed 99 cavalrymen one of the army's worst defeats of the Indian wars. Perry lost about a third of his command—34 dead. Not a single Nez Percé was killed.

News of what the press promptly dubbed a massacre shocked Howard and panicked white settlements across the Northwest. Rumors flew. Among them was a false report that Looking Glass, a well-known chief who had thus far kept his own band of non-treaty Nez Percé at peace, was recruiting warriors for the fleeing Nez Percé. Howard's soldiers savagely attacked Looking Glass's innocent village, killing some of his people. The enraged chief and his neighbor, Red Owl, both promptly cast their lot with their retreating fellow tribesmen.

The nontreaty Indians were now at peak strength, with more than 200 fighting men. They included some of the Nez Percé's most respected warriors—Looking Glass, young Ollokot, the aged veteran Toohoolhoolzote, and the seasoned Plains fighters Rainbow and Five Wounds. War parties under their bold leadership repeatedly bested Howard's patrols over the following days, frustrating his determined efforts to round up the Indians.

By July 6, the noncombatants of the five bands were camped together near the south fork of the Clearwater River. They rested and grazed their stock there until the afternoon of July 11, when the army burst in on them with volleys of cannon shot and a rain of Gatling gun fire. Reacting swiftly, the Nez Percé warriors besieged Howard's 600 men, pinning them down for nearly 30 hours while the old men, women, and children, led by Joseph and the elderly White Bird, made their escape north, abandoning most of their possessions. The warriors followed in their wake, keeping the army at bay.

Although the Nez Percé remained beyond his grasp, Howard declared victory at Clearwater and deflected public criticism of the earlier debacle at White Bird Canyon by wrongly attributing the Indians' success there to the purported military genius of Chief Joseph, the best known of the Nez Percé chiefs and widely assumed to be their leader. The press began to call the campaign Chief Joseph's War.

All yesterday fighting; all this morning they did not crowd us. But now, meeting no Indian bullets, they came charging bravely.

- YELLOW WOLF

SITE OF THE CLEARWATER BATTLE

I tried to surrender in Idaho, but my offer was rejected. The soldiers came upon my camp, and the first thing I knew, the bullets were flying around.

— LOOKING GLASS

WEIPPE PRAIRIE, IDAHO

Looking Glass strongly counseled peace until goaded into combat by the unwarranted attack on his people in their Idaho homes.

> *We traveled through the Bitterroot Valley slowly. The white people were friendly. We did much buying and trading with them. No more fighting! We had left General Howard and his war in Idaho.*
>
> — YELLOW WOLF

BITTERROOT MOUNTAINS FROM THE LOLO TRAIL

Following Nez Percé traditions of band autonomy, the Indians' plans thus far had been worked out by the various chiefs meeting in council. But after the battle of Clearwater, the chiefs decided to coordinate their movements more closely and to designate one man as their guide. Convening on July 15 at Weippe Prairie, they voted to cross the Bitterroot Mountains into Montana, where they hoped to find refuge among the friendly Crow; Howard's command ended at the Idaho border, and they believed he would not pursue them beyond it. Looking Glass, who had often traveled the Lolo Trail through the mountains and had close ties with the Crow, was elected guide.

Driving a herd of more than 2,000 horses, the fugitives started up the rugged 100-mile trail on July 16, picking their way through undergrowth and uprooted trees. They emerged on the Montana side nine days later to find their way blocked by a log barricade manned by 35 soldiers, 200 civilian volunteers, and a few local Salish Indians. Looking Glass, Joseph, and White Bird rode forward to ask permission to pass, promising they would not harm the people of Montana. The soldiers refused. But the volunteers and the Salish, unwilling to provoke the Nez Percé, abandoned their posts. The next morning, the soldiers looked on helplessly as the Nez Percé traversed a

high ridge just out of rifle range and skirted their barricade—derisively labeled "Fort Fizzle" by the settlers.

As the Nez Percé turned south through the Bitterroot Valley, they began to take heart. There were no signs of soldiers, and the whites seemed friendly; many even sold supplies to the Indians. On August 7, the Indians crossed the hills at the head of the Bitterroot and entered the Big Hole Valley. Some of the Nez Percé were anxious and wanted to press on eastward to Crow country. But Looking Glass called for a halt so that they could rest, hunt, and cut new lodgepoles to replace those they had been forced to leave on the Clearwater battlefield.

Bullets were singing through the tipi, splintering the poles. . . shouts and war whoops mingled with the firing, and children and women were crying.

- TWO MOONS

A REPLICA OF GIBBON'S HOWITZER AT BIG HOLE

As the Nez Percé made their peaceful way through Montana, 163 infantrymen under the command of Colonel John Gibbon were en route from Missoula to intercept them. Early on August 9, Gibbon's men stormed into the sleeping Indian camp, clubbing and shooting terrified women and children. Rallying, the Indians drove the soldiers back but suffered terrible losses. More than 60 people, mostly women and children, were killed and many more wounded. Twelve warriors died, among them the revered Rainbow and Five Wounds—a devastating loss.

The weeping Nez Percé laid their dead in shallow graves hastily clawed into a streambed and tied their wounded to travois. At noon, Joseph and White Bird hurried the families and the pony herd south, leaving the warriors behind to fight Gibbon. General Howard—who had been delayed getting his artillery across the Lolo Trail—arrived the following day to find Gibbon's command in tatters; the Indians had even managed to capture and dismantle his howitzer before breaking away to rejoin their families.

But their plight was desperate. Although Howard fell several days behind, other troops were closing in from the north and east. On September 13, Colonel Samuel Sturgis along with 400 cavalrymen caught up to the band at a place called Canyon Creek. Rising once more to the occasion, the warriors took advantage of the terrain and held off Sturgis's force while their people escaped onto the plains. There a new enemy appeared: Bannock and Crow scouts raided the strung-out Nez Percé column, stealing horses and picking off and scalping wounded stragglers.

The hostility of the Crow was a final crushing blow. The Nez Percé knew now there would be no help from their old buffalo-hunting friends. Their last hope lay in Canada, where they might find refuge among Sitting Bull's Sioux, who were camped there in exile after defeating Lieutenant Colonel George Armstrong Custer a year earlier at the Battle of the Little Bighorn.

SITE OF THE CANYON CREEK SKIRMISH

SURRENDER AT BEAR'S PAW

You have seen hail sometime... the bullet hail. Most of our... as leaves before the storm...

WHERE TOOHOOLHOOLZOTE FELL AT BEAR'S PAW

On September 29, the tired fugitives reached the Bear's Paw Mountains, 40 miles from Canada. Unaware that Colonel Nelson A. Miles and 383 men were only hours away, they stopped to rest and kill buffalo for food and robes. The next day, Miles attacked.

In this, their last battle, the Nez Percé exacted a heavy toll. But many of their own men died, including Toohoolhoolzote and Ollokot. Miles surrounded the camp as a bitter storm blew in. On October 4, Looking Glass was shot. Only two chiefs were left alive. The defiant White Bird slipped through enemy lines at night with some fugitives who accompanied him to Canada. But Joseph remained with those who were weary of the chase and yielded to Miles. "It is cold, and we have no blankets. The little children are freezing," he said. "I am tired; my heart is sick and sad. From where the sun now stands, I will fight no more forever."

The flight of the Nez Percé had aroused sympathy, and Miles promised that those who surrendered would be sent to the Idaho reservation. Instead, they were packed off to Kansas and Oklahoma, where many died. Eventually, some joined the Nez Percé in Idaho, but Joseph's Wallowa band was kept apart. "The earth is the mother of all people, and all people should have equal rights upon it," Joseph implored in 1879—to no avail. His people were moved to Washington State's Colville Reservation. Joseph died there in 1904. The cause of death, reported the agency doctor, was a broken heart.

...veling the grass. Indians were so leveled by
warriors left from the Big Hole had been swept
Chief Ollokot, Lone Bird, and Lean Elk were gone...

- YELLOW WOLF

General Miles had promised that we might return
to our country with what stock we had left. I
thought we could start again. I believed General
Miles, or I never would have surrendered.

- CHIEF JOSEPH

BEAR'S PAW BATTLEFIELD

4

PATRIOTS IN THE WESTERN WARS

Red Cloud, who counted 80 coups in a lifetime of fighting, rose to prominence as war chief of the Iteshicha, or Bad Faces, band of the Oglala Sioux tribe. He continually frustrated the U.S. Army in the 1860s, forcing the government to offer a treaty. In peacetime he served as the civil chief of his band.

Red Cloud, war leader of the powerful Oglala Sioux, received the news in the winter of 1866. The Great Father at Washington was sending a commission of high-ranking emissaries to Fort Laramie on the North Platte River in present-day Wyoming, and inviting tribes for hundreds of miles around—the Sioux, the Northern Cheyenne, and the Arapaho—to attend a parley of major importance in June, the Moon of Making Fat. Together, said the Great Father's spokesmen, the white man and the red man would smoke the pipe of a just and lasting peace, and there would be grand feasts and mountains of gifts for all.

Washington was anxious to propitiate the Plains Indians, if it was possible. The Civil War had ended at last, and President Andrew Johnson's administration was busy with the affairs of Reconstruction. The government had little desire for continuing battle in the West—particularly against the ferocious Sioux and their allies. Yet Johnson and his advisers also knew that nothing on this earth could stop the wild, westering stampede of settlers from the overcrowded East to the limitless lands and riches beyond the Mississippi River. It was clear: The Indians were an obstacle, and one way or another, they had to be removed.

At immediate issue were gold deposits discovered in the early 1860s near the headwaters of the Missouri River in the southwestern corner of Montana Territory. The fastest route to the gold strike was the Bozeman Trail, an offshoot of the Oregon Trail leading northwest from Fort Laramie. But the trail cut across the prime hunting grounds of the Powder River country, threatening the buffalo and lesser game that the Indians relied upon for food. In angry consequence, Red Cloud and the other war chiefs had made the route virtually impassable with their incessant ambushes. Now, in exchange for gifts and vows of peace, Washington hoped to secure a right of way through the Indian lands to the gold fields. Just in case that proposal failed, Colonel Henry Carrington and 700 men would shortly arrive to build forts and provide protection for white travelers.

At the parley in Soldiers' Town, as the Sioux called Fort Laramie, Red

Cloud spoke of his desire for peace, but he warned that it was up to the whites to maintain it. E. B. Taylor, head of the Northern Superintendency for the Bureau of Indian Affairs, assured Red Cloud that the Great Father wanted no more Indian land. All he asked was permission to retain a simple trail to the gold-mining camps—a trail no wider than the space that a "wagon would take between the wheels." The white travelers, Taylor solemnly promised, would be forbidden to disturb the game. In exchange, the Americans would provide the Indians with generous annuities.

Red Cloud and the other chiefs found the offer tempting. The winter had been harsh, and their people were hungry. The Indian leaders asked for an adjournment so they could travel back to their camps some 50 miles away and win their communities' approval. But when the Indians returned and negotiations resumed on June 13, Red Cloud's goodwill abruptly evaporated. On that very day, Colonel Carrington marched into Fort Laramie at the head of his soldiers.

The arrival of troops during the peace negotiations infuriated the Oglala war chief. Red Cloud refused to be introduced to Carrington and launched into an impassioned speech, accusing the Americans of deceit, of pretending to negotiate for land that they all along intended to take by force. "The Great Father sends us presents and wants us to sell him the road," one observer recalled Red Cloud saying, "but the white chief goes with soldiers to steal the road before the Indians say yes or no."

Unfazed by Red Cloud's protest, Taylor proceeded to sign up the other participants. They included Spotted Tail, leader of the Sicangu or Brulé (Burnt Thigh) Sioux, who lived south of the Powder River and thus had no interest in the region; a few compliant Cheyennes; and a handful of so-called stay-around-the-fort Indians, who had forsaken their traditional ways in exchange for easy access to the white man's goods and provisions. By this time, Red Cloud and his entourage had already struck their tipis and departed, refusing all of the government's gifts. Red Cloud left with a dire prediction for Carrington's contingent of troopers. "In two moons," he vowed, "the command will not have a hoof left." It was a prophecy he would come shockingly close to fulfilling.

By the mid-1860s, the campaign to confine the Indians and resettle the West with whites had been under way for more than two decades. California, Nevada, Oregon, and Texas had achieved statehood, and much of the remaining land west of the Missouri River had been organized into territories. The great tidal wave of white civilization that had uprooted

Red Cloud's special civil leader's shirt consists of deerskin decorated with paint, blue and white beads, porcupine quills, and trailing fringes of human hair. The shirt symbolized Red Cloud's leadership status; the fringes of hair represented the people he cared for and led.

the eastern woodlands Indians and deposited more than 80,000 of them on shoddy reservations beyond the Mississippi was now crashing onto the domain of the some 75,000 nomadic buffalo hunters, who ranged from central Texas north to the Canadian provinces.

As early as 1853, Thomas Fitzpatrick, a U.S. Indian agent for the Platte and Arkansas river country, noted the cataclysmic effect of the endless streams of covered wagons that were crawling over the Oregon Trail. The Indians, he wrote, "are in abject want of food half the year. The travel upon the road drives the buffalo off or else confines them in a narrow path during the period of migration, and the different tribes are forced to contend with hostile nations in seeking support for their villages. Their women are pinched with want, and their children are constantly crying with hunger." An assessment made just over a decade later by Brigadier General John Pope, commander of the Department of the Northwest, was just as bleak. The United States, Pope declared, was "at one grasp seizing the whole region of the country occupied by the Indians and plunging them without warning into suffering and starvation."

Faced with this desperate problem, the Plains tribes turned to their war chiefs, men who in different times might have wielded far less influence. The crisis called forth scores of Indian patriots with different strategies to save their people. But none were more illustrious than Red Cloud of the Oglala Sioux, Washakie of the Eastern Shoshone, and Quanah Parker, the gray-eyed, half-white leader of the fearsome Comanche. Washakie chose the path of friendship and cooperation with the whites. Quanah opted for war and then, when that became hopeless, turned to diplomacy. Red Cloud's course was also war. In the end, however, he too would be brought to terms with the federal government. But first his warriors would inflict a number of calamitous defeats on the white nemesis.

At the time of the Fort Laramie peace council, Red Cloud had already lived a lifetime full of achievement. Although details of his birth and childhood are sketchy, it is generally acknowledged that he was born in present-day Nebraska in 1822, near the spot where the Platte River divides into a north and a south fork. According to some accounts, his parents died when Red Cloud, or Mahpiua Luta, as the Oglala called him, was still a small boy, and he was raised by his mother's brother, Old Smoke, leader of an Oglala band known as the Bad Faces.

When Red Cloud was only 15, he began riding with war parties against the Pawnee, Crow, Ute, Omaha, and Shoshone—traditional enemies of the Sioux. The next year, he took his first scalp. In subsequent forays, the young warrior demonstrated not only bravery but also cunning. On one occasion, he and a Miniconjou warrior located a Crow camp and made off with 50 horses; another time, he risked death by charging three Crow warriors and counting coup by striking them with his bow. Red Cloud's reputation as a titan in combat was ensured at age 20 when he shot Bull Bear, the leader of a rival band of Oglalas, in a community dispute. Shortly afterward, he led his first war party—a horse-stealing raid against the Pawnee. The young warrior suffered a deep arrow wound below his ribs but miraculously survived—proof that his medicine was indeed powerful. Henceforth, Red Cloud was a celebrated leader of warriors. Tradition maintains that by the time his fighting days were over, about 1868, he had counted coup 80 times.

Not long after Red Cloud angrily led his warriors away from the peace council at Fort Laramie in June of 1866, his scouts brought in alarming news. The *wasichus,* as the Sioux called the white men, had advanced well over 200 miles from Fort Laramie northwest on the Bozeman Trail to the fork of Big Piney and Little Piney creeks, tributaries of the Powder River, and were chopping down trees to build a stockade. Named Fort Phil Kearny after a Union general who was killed during the Civil War, the stockade was to serve as Carrington's headquarters. Soon after it was built, Carrington dispatched two companies of infantry to the Bighorn River, 90 miles farther northwest, to build another outpost on the Bozeman Trail—Fort C. F. Smith. Meanwhile, other workers were busy strengthening Fort Reno, built on the trail two years earlier, about 175 miles northwest of Fort Laramie.

In the early fall, Red Cloud sent runners to the scattered bands of Oglala and Miniconjou Sioux, and to his Cheyenne and Arapaho allies, summoning them to a council after they had completed their communal buffalo hunts. By December, some 4,000 warriors had gathered along the Tongue River, one day's march north of Fort Phil Kearny. Decades later, Black Elk, an Oglala holy man who was a child at the time, recalled Red Cloud's encampment as being so vast that a man on horseback "could ride through our villages from sunrise until the day was above his head."

Carrington and his superiors did not appreciate the danger his command faced. True, there had been a number of minor Indian attacks during the summer. But a U.S. Army inspector dismissed them as "depredations of a desultory, thieving nature." Carrington himself, although anxious for more men and ammunition, remained confident that his troops were prepared for the worst. "Red Cloud does not comprehend the idea of a year's supplies," he cheerfully reported in November of 1866, "nor that we are now prepared to not only pass the winter, but next spring and summer, even if he takes the offensive."

That same month, Carrington received his reinforcements—one cavalry company and a number of officers, including a fire-eating Civil War veteran named Captain William J. Fetterman. There was much talk among the new men of bringing back Red Cloud's scalp. Fetterman himself boasted: "Give me 80 men, and I'll ride through the whole Sioux nation." His foolhardiness would soon play directly into Red Cloud's hands.

On December 6, a small party of Sioux attacked one of Carrington's woodcutting crews in the hills a few miles northwest of Fort Phil Kearny. Riding to the rescue, Fetterman led a force composed of cavalry and mounted infantry directly into an ambush that left two soldiers dead and several wounded. The successful skirmish gave Red Cloud an idea. Having seen how easily the whites could be tricked, he decided to use the same ploy again, only this time he would set a massive trap. He selected 10 of his best warriors, including the 19-year-old Crazy Horse, to act as decoys. Their job would be to attack the next party of woodcutters that left the fort in order to draw out another company of soldiers. The decoys would lure the soldiers up and over a spur, known to the whites as Lodge Trail Ridge. There Red Cloud's full complement of warriors would be lying in wait, concealed behind boulders and tall grass.

Red Cloud's opportunity came on the icy morning of December 21. At about 11 o'clock, the Indians spied a team of loggers rumbling toward a cluster of pines off to the west. Exactly as planned, the decoys pounced, and the army lookout issued an alarm. Again, Fetterman rode out to the rescue, this time at the head of a combined force of some 80 infantrymen and cavalrymen. Carrington had given him explicit orders: "Support the wood train. Relieve it and report to me. Do not engage or pursue Indians at its expense. Under no circumstances pursue over Lodge Trail Ridge."

Instead of heading straight for the logging party, Fetterman veered north to prevent the Indians from escaping across Lodge Trail Ridge. As Fetterman approached the ridge, Crazy Horse and the other decoys galloped in front of him with whoops and taunts. When the captain halted, the Indians redoubled their efforts, one warrior actually riding in among the soldiers. At this, Fetterman ordered his men to charge. As the Amer-

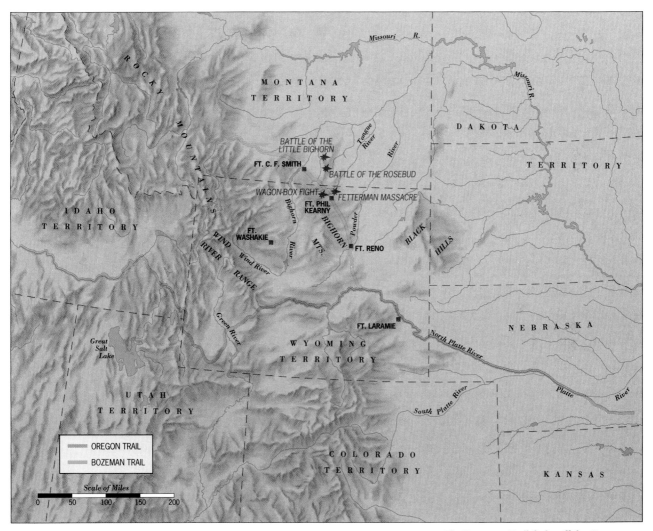

The Bozeman Trail forks off the Oregon Trail northwest of Fort Laramie in the map above, cutting through the Sioux buffalo hunting grounds in Wyoming and Montana on its way to gold fields in Montana. Through a series of brilliant hit-and-run attacks, Red Cloud and his allies forced the U.S. government to abandon Forts C. F. Smith, Phil Kearny, and Reno along the Bozeman Trail in 1868. That same year, Washakie and the Eastern Shoshone were given a three-million-acre reservation in the Wind River valley, a reward for their friendship with trappers, settlers, and soldiers.

icans blundered over the ridge and into the valley beyond, the decoys gave a prearranged signal: Half of them circled in one direction, half in the other. Instantly, hundreds of warriors sprang from their hiding places, raining torrents of arrows down on the soldiers, then rushing in to brain them with war clubs and hatchets.

Fire Thunder, a 16-year-old Oglala, was among the ambushers. "We heard a shot up over the hill, and we knew the soldiers were coming," he recalled. "So we held the noses of our ponies that they might not whinny at the soldiers' horses. Soon we saw our men coming back, and some of them were walking and leading their horses, so that the soldiers would think they were worn out. Then the men we had sent ahead came running down the road between us, and the soldiers on horseback followed them, shooting. When they came to the flat at the bottom of the hill, the fighting began all at once. There were many bullets, but there were more arrows—so many that it was like a cloud of grasshoppers. The soldiers were falling all the while they were fighting up the hill. We were told to crawl up on them, and we did. When we were close, someone yelled: 'Let us go! This is a good day to die. Think of the helpless ones at home!'"

Hearing the sounds of battle, Carrington hastily dispatched Captain Tenedor Ten Eyck and a relief force of 54 men. But by the time Ten Eyck reached the ridge, the firing had ended. In the valley below, some 2,000 warriors were riding away. Fetterman and his entire force lay dead. The fighting had lasted scarcely 30 minutes.

At dusk Ten Eyck rode down to the killing ground. It was blanketed with corpses—stripped, scalped, and horribly mutilated so as to deny the dead, according to Indian belief, whole bodies in the afterlife. "I give you some of the facts as to my men," Carrington wrote grimly to his superiors two weeks later. "Eyes torn out and laid on rocks; noses cut off; ears cut off; chins hewn off; teeth chopped out; joints of fingers, brains taken out and placed on rocks with other members of the body; entrails taken out and exposed; hands cut off, arms taken from sockets." Fetterman was found with a bullet hole in his temple—evidently he had committed suicide, or had been dispatched by a fellow officer, to avoid capture. Even a dog that had followed the soldiers lay dead, bristling with arrows. Only one body was left undisturbed—that of the middle-aged bugler, one Adolph Metzger. It was found tenderly cloaked in a buffalo robe as a sign of respect. Weaponless, Metzger had apparently gone down fighting, using his bugle as a club, an act of courage the Indians recognized by allowing him the dignified death of a warrior. White men called the fight the Fet-

A stately Red Cloud wears an elegant outfit of European-style clothes in a portrait made while he was visiting the Carlisle Indian School in Pennsylvania in 1880. A negotiator for Indian rights after the era of war, Red Cloud made a number of trips east to discuss affairs with the White Father in Washington.

terman Massacre; it became known among the Sioux as the Battle of the Hundred Slain, after the number of bluecoats that a medicine man fore-told would be delivered into the Indians' trap.

Over the next year and a half, Red Cloud kept up the pressure on the Bozeman Trail, raiding at every opportunity. The garrisons of the three Bozeman Trail forts became virtual prisoners inside the walls of their own stockades. Any white that dared to venture along the trail placed his life in jeopardy. In one foray, Red Cloud and a thousand or more warriors attacked a heavily armed woodcutting camp outside Fort Phil Kearny. Be-cause the camp was formed by a circle of wagons minus their wheels and bases, the clash became known as the Wagon-Box Fight. Shouting their shrill war cries, the Sioux horsemen galloped their ponies around and

Invoking the power of the buffalo, Sitting Bull painted the stark yellow image of the animal on this unusual box drum. A dedicated singer of songs, the chief used the drum for accompaniment.

Holy man and leader of the Hunkpapa Sioux, Sitting Bull is shown addressing a forum on tribal matters. Between 1883 and 1890, Sitting Bull met with federal officials and tribal emissaries to debate government policy regarding the reservation.

around the oval, waiting for an opportunity to charge. But the Americans, armed with new breechloading repeating rifles, drove them off. After regrouping, the Indians tried to storm the camp on foot. Hundreds of warriors crawled to within a few yards of the defenses only to be driven off by fire from the "medicine guns." Although Red Cloud's forces had to retreat, they captured many army horses. More important, they had once again demonstrated their resolve to keep the Bozeman Trail impassable.

By the spring of 1868, President Andrew Johnson and the U.S. Congress had exhausted their patience. With the army committed to overseeing Reconstruction in the South and tied down in the West guarding the Union Pacific Railroad work crews, the continuation of a war with the Sioux over the Bozeman Trail seemed particularly senseless. Besides, once the railroad was completed, a rail spur to the gold fields of Montana would greatly diminish the importance of the contested overland trail. Washington prepared yet another treaty and tried to induce the Sioux to sign. They offered lavish gifts, and many chiefs did put their marks on the document. But Red Cloud remained obdurate. The word went out from his camp: "We are on the mountains overlooking the soldiers and the forts. When we see the soldiers moving away and the forts abandoned, then I will come down and talk."

In July the Americans met Red Cloud's demand. While he and his warriors watched from the hills, the garrison at Fort C. F. Smith departed the compound, carrying what they could on their horses and leaving the rest behind. At dawn the next day, Red Cloud and his men rode down and burned the fort to the ground. Before the week was out, the Americans evacuated Forts Phil Kearny and Reno. Red Cloud had won his war, but he was in no hurry to establish a formal truce; he waited until after the autumn hunting season before traveling to Fort Laramie. He arrived in November, heading a huge force of Hunkpapa, Sihasapa, Sicangu, and Itazipco Sioux, including some 125 lesser chiefs. To honor his success, the Sioux had conferred on him the right to make peace for all of them.

At first, Red Cloud haughtily refused to shake hands with the whites, offering only to touch fingertips. But at last, after several days of negotiations, he washed his hands with dust from the floor and put his mark on the treaty. At one point, Red Cloud gazed up at the sky. He remarked that when he had come to Fort Laramie two years earlier, a heavy cloud hung overhead, presaging war. Now the heavens were a cloudless blue.

In essence, the accord created a huge reservation for the Sioux in Dakota Territory stretching from the Missouri River to the Black Hills. It also established specific agencies where the various bands were to receive government rations and where trading with the whites would take place. The Oglala were ordered to a spot on the Missouri, far from their beloved Powder River. Red Cloud had no intention of making a new home in this inhospitable region. "I signed a treaty of peace," he later told government officials, "but it was not this treaty. This one is all lies!"

Red Cloud did not go to live on the reservation as he had been ordered, but remained in the Powder River country. In 1870 he paid the first of several visits to Washington to plead his case before President Grant. While there, Red Cloud conducted himself with a dignity that impressed official Washington. He was shown ample evidence of American military might—including the firing of a 15-inch coastal gun—but the Oglala chief

Yellow, blue, and red medicine symbols adorn this deerskin shield cover thought to have belonged to Crazy Horse, who fought under Red Cloud. A witness to the carnage wrought by U.S. Army attacks on Indian villages in his youth, Crazy Horse mistrusted all whites and despised their ways.

remained firm. He would not move to the Missouri; instead, he proposed a compromise, requesting permission to make his base on the Platte River, closer to home territory. "The white men have surrounded me and have left me nothing but an island," he complained. "When we first had this land, we were strong. Now our nation is melting away like snow on the hillside where the sun is warm; while the white people grow like the blades of grass when summer is coming."

Red Cloud's mission to Washington was briefly successful. Upon his return, the Oglala were given an agency on the Platte, 32 miles downstream of Fort Laramie. But over the next few years, the government used every means short of force to compel Red Cloud and his people to move north to the reservation on the Missouri. Red Cloud held out until 1876—the year war broke out anew with the whites. Again, the issue was gold—"the yellow metal that the wasichus worship and that makes them crazy." It had been discovered in the Black Hills several years before, and the

Americans were now bent on getting the Sioux to give up the region—even though they had ceded it to the Indians for "as long as grass should grow and water flow." The hostile Sioux who refused to repair to the reservation were led by other great warriors—Crazy Horse and Big Road of the Oglala; Sitting Bull, Gall, Black Moon, and Crow King of the Hunk-papa; Spotted Eagle of the Itazipco; Hump and Fast Bull of the Miniconjou. Red Cloud played no role in the fighting, although some of his followers, including his son Jack, may have participated in the defeat of Custer's 7th Cavalry at Little Bighorn. In the aftermath, at the U.S. government's behest, Red Cloud led a group of 100 warriors that tracked down Crazy Horse and persuaded him to surrender.

Red Cloud lived out the remainder of his days on the reservation. When younger warriors criticized him for succumbing to white ways, he reminded them that, because of his efforts, his people had retained for many years the right to hunt in their beloved Powder River territory. The once-mighty chief's face bespoke a lifetime of struggle. As he grew old, his high, broad brow was deeply furrowed, and his stern mouth sagged at the corners. Red Cloud's hair, dark and luxuriant until he was nearly 60, finally turned white. His vision was poor. Instead of the fringed buckskins and feathers of his early life, the old chief most often donned a shirt and vest. In his old age, Red Cloud would certainly have agreed with what one old Sioux said of the white man: "They made us many promises, more than I can remember, but they never kept but one. They promised to take our land, and they took it." Red Cloud died in 1909 at the age of 87.

Red Cloud had lived two-thirds of his life before he concluded that armed resistance to the white invaders was futile. But a few leaders of tribes less powerful than the Sioux decided early on that an alliance with the whites offered their people the best hope of survival. Warfare was a way of life on the Plains, and weaker tribes were accustomed to joining forces with others against a common foe. When the white men came, it was quickly apparent that they would make the most powerful allies of all. Thus, fighting with the newcomers rather than against them became the chosen path for the Pawnee, the Crow, and the Ute. But none of them made a greater effort to cooperate than the Eastern Shoshone, under the leadership of the chief Washakie. Tragically, his policy of accommodation produced an outcome scarcely more beneficial to his people than Red Cloud's intransigence produced for the Sioux.

Like the two other major groups of the Shoshone people, the North-

Acknowledged even by enemy Indians to be a great warrior, Chief Washakie of the Shoshone wears the feathered war bonnet that he possessed during the time he helped the U.S. Army fight off Crazy Horse's warriors at the Battle of the Rosebud.

ern and Western, the Eastern Shoshone share ancient ties with the Ute and Paiute to the south and west and the distant Comanche of the southern Plains. But in contrast to their neighboring kin who drew more of their sustenance from the mountains, many Eastern Shoshones had long since adopted the way of the buffalo hunters. This shift reinforced the independence of Washakie's people from the rest of the Shoshones, yet at the same time exposed them to relentless attacks by other Plains tribes. Together, this distinctiveness and the desperate need for allies paved the way for a deep amiability with the whites.

By the mid-19th century, the Eastern Shoshone were hard pressed by the Blackfeet, Crow, Cheyenne, Sioux, and Arapaho, but they were themselves fierce fighters—none fiercer than Washakie himself. Washakie spent his youth learning the art of combat. For several years, he lived among a band of Bannocks— Paiutes who had taken up residence with the Northern Shoshone. He then joined a band of Eastern Shoshones living along the Green River in southwestern Wyoming, where he soon established a terrifying reputation. Once, after a Blackfeet war party stole some Shoshone ponies, he and two other tribesmen relentlessly tracked the raiders some 600 miles, finally overtaking them on the Missouri River in Montana. They not only recovered the entire herd but also brought back the scalps of most of the Blackfeet. In another skirmish with the Blackfeet, Washakie took an arrow through the left cheek. The wound earned him the nickname Scar Face.

By the 1840s, he was a legendary figure. Osborne Russell, a trapper who lived eight years in the Wyoming country, reported other Shoshone warriors boasting of his exploits. The Blackfeet, they said, "quaked in fear" at the mention of Washakie's name. Many years later, Washakie reflected upon his early deeds. "As a young man I delighted in war," he recalled. "When my tribe was at peace, I would wander off sometimes alone in search of an enemy. I am ashamed to speak of these years, for I killed a great many Indians."

The Eastern Shoshone history of friendship with whites dates back to

The Wind River flows through the rich landscape of western Wyoming, long a home of the Shoshone. Chief Washakie, who especially loved the valley, persuaded the U.S. government to grant his tribe nearly three million acres of the Wind River region; it remains an Indian reservation, which the Shoshone now share with the Arapaho.

1805 when the Lemhi band, to which Washakie's mother probably belonged, provided food, horses, and guides to the explorers Meriwether Lewis and William Clark. Traveling with the Americans was a 16-year-old Shoshone girl named Sacajawea, who served as the group's interpreter. Washakie was a child at the time. Several decades later, when white fur trappers and traders began coming into the area, the Eastern Shoshone welcomed them too. And with good reason. The Shoshone were constantly threatened by hostile neighbors—the Crow and Blackfeet to the north, and the Sioux, Cheyenne, and Arapaho to the east. The whites not only provided the Eastern Shoshone with guns and ammunition to defend

themselves but sometimes fought alongside them as well. In one major battle in 1826, some 300 whites and Shoshone warriors cornered a large number of Blackfeet in a canyon in Utah, killing 173.

Umbrella-carrying warriors are among a delegation of Indians sent by Chief Washakie to welcome President Chester A. Arthur to the Shoshone Wind River country in 1883. Instead of arranging for a neutral meeting place, Washakie insisted that the president be brought to his encampment.

Each year, Washakie and his fellow tribesmen gathered with the whites for a trade fair. The Shoshone exchanged their beaver pelts for firearms, ammunition, clothing, tobacco, whiskey, and other trade goods. The warriors played games, danced, and showed off their horsemanship, while the trappers vied with them and with one another in contests of strength or marksmanship. The missionary Father Pierre-Jean De Smet wrote of one Shoshone performance: "Three hundred of their warriors came up in good order and at full gallop into the midst of our camp. They were hideously painted, armed with war clubs, and covered all over with feathers, pearls, wolves' tails, teeth and claws of animals, and outlandish ornaments. Those who had wounds received in war, and those who had killed the enemies of their tribe, displayed their scars ostentatiously and waved the scalps they had taken on the ends of poles. After riding a few times around the camp, uttering at intervals shouts of joy, they dismounted and all came to shake hands with the whites in sign of friendship."

The last trade fairs were held in the early 1840s. The once-plentiful beaver had been overhunted, and their pelts were now scarce. The dawn of the new decade also signaled change among the Eastern Shoshone. For some time, the tribe had been unhappy with their principal chief, Hiding Bear, and a movement was afoot to transfer allegiance to his brother. In 1842 Hiding Bear died suddenly; the following year his brother also

passed away. For a brief period, the Eastern Shoshone scattered into small bands with no strong leader to unite them. As had been the case in the past, pressure from hostile tribes brought them back together, and they coalesced around their best warrior—Washakie. Within a few years, the new chief, now in his forties, headed a band whose core territory lay in the valleys of the Green and Wind rivers, with hunting grounds spreading all the way across most of present-day western Wyoming. Washakie ruled his band with an iron hand, and even the headmen of other bands bowed to his authority when they were traveling or fighting together.

Despite many challenges, Washakie led the Eastern Shoshone for nearly 60 years. The rules of membership in his band were clear. There would be no violence against whites; those who thought otherwise had to leave. So deep was Washakie's conviction in this matter that he once threatened to kill one of his own sons rather than see him take up arms against the Americans. Late in his life, Washakie overheard a group of Shoshones complaining that he lacked courage because of his unwillingness to resist the whites. Controlling his anger, Washakie bided his time, then one evening, packed a few items and left camp on his horse. When he returned, he carried seven fresh scalps. "Let him who can do a greater feat than this claim the chieftaincy," said the old warrior. No one rose to the challenge, and the whispers about Washakie's courage ceased.

His Shoshone tribesmen earned the undying gratitude of travelers along the Oregon Trail by offering them shelter from the elements and protection against hostile tribes. Many years later, veterans of the dangerous passage presented Washakie with a paper signed by 9,000 people, attesting to his support. Once, during a severe blizzard, a group of travelers limped into Washakie's camp, half-frozen. One man could not walk. Washakie ordered one of the women in his band to nestle the man's feet in her bosom. After 24 hours of this gently warming treatment, the man was able to leave Washakie's camp on foot.

By the late 1850s, however, such generosity toward the whites was a rare event. Trappers, whose wild, solitary ways sat well with the Indians, were soon replaced by swarms of settlers streaming west along the Oregon Trail, leaving in their wake spoiled rivers and barren hunting grounds. With their outrage compounded by the frequent failure of the government to come up with the promised compensation for loss of land or grants of right of way, many Shoshones, Bannocks, and Paiutes struck back. Even Washakie found it difficult to restrain his warriors, commenting to one white trader that unless the government improved its treatment of his people, he would let his warriors steal all they wanted.

Through several years of bloody raids and skirmishes, Washakie managed to keep his people out of the fray. But war fever finally proved irresistible, especially when so many outposts, settlements, and wagon trains were left almost defenseless with the departure of the soldiers for the Civil War. Early in 1862, hundreds of his Eastern Shoshones were lured away by Pashego, the militant, charismatic chief of the Bannocks, who had earlier called Washakie an "old woman" for his aversion to fighting the whites. In March they attacked all along the Oregon and Overland Stage trails, running off or capturing virtually all the livestock but taking only one life, as if still under the powerful sway of Washakie.

Fighting continued through the rest of the year, but most of the Eastern Shoshones stayed on the sidelines, while the Bannocks and other Shoshones farther west continued their raids. But after scores of whites had been cut down in a series of massacres, the army sent in a detachment of volunteers, well armed and several hundred strong, to suppress the hostiles. In January 1863, the soldiers cornered the Northern Shoshone chief Bear Hunter and his band in a ravine near the Bear River, about 140 miles north of Salt Lake City. After a one-sided, four-hour battle, the chief and more than 200 of his people lay dead in the snow. Word of the slaughter spread quickly through the region, persuading all but a handful of warriors to give up the fight. Washakie's policy of coexistence was vindicated, and his star rose, never again to set among his people.

By now the Wyoming country was filling up with settlers. Each year

An honor guard of the 1st U.S. Cavalry (background) escorts the flag-draped coffin of centenarian Chief Washakie during the full military funeral that followed his death in February 1900. The inscription on the granite monument erected by the War Department read, in part: "Always loyal to the government and to his white brothers."

there were fewer and fewer buffalo. Concerned for his people's survival, Washakie began to press for a permanent reservation. In 1868 the U.S. government agreed to his request, setting aside almost three million acres in the Wind River valley and agreeing to provide each Shoshone family with a plot of farmland, along with seeds and tools.

But it would be several years before Washakie could move his band onto the land. His old Indian enemies were the cause. In 1868 Red Cloud made peace with the whites in exchange for evacuation of the Bozeman Trail forts. But the treaty Red Cloud signed did not prevent his warriors and their Cheyenne and Arapaho allies from continuing to attack the Shoshone. Fearing he would be unable to defend the Wind River land

against their assaults, Washakie persuaded U.S. Army officials to build a military post—Camp Brown—on the reservation. The American military presence on Shoshone land had the desired effect. In July of 1874, when Sioux, Cheyenne, and Arapaho war parties threatened to attack, Washakie and a force of cavalrymen launched a preemptive strike against an Arapaho camp, killing at least 25 and ending the peril. Two years later, in 1876, when the U.S. Army embarked on a campaign to subdue Crazy Horse, Sitting Bull, and the other hostile Sioux, Cheyenne, and Arapaho leaders, Washakie sent warriors to fight alongside the Americans and their Indian allies, including the Crow. Although the Crow and the Shoshone were traditional enemies, and Washakie had once killed a Crow chief in single combat, the two tribes made peace with each other in order to confront their common enemy, the Sioux.

In June of 1876, Washakie's force of about 120 warriors, along with a like number of Crows under the chiefs Old Crow, Medicine Crow, and Good Heart, helped save General George Crook and his force of more than 1,000 men from the fate suffered by Captain William Fetterman's troops 10 years earlier. On a campaign against the Sioux, Crook's soldiers had crossed the Tongue River on June 16, reaching the headwaters of Rosebud Creek the next day. There Shoshone and Crow scouts discovered several thousand Sioux, led by Crazy Horse, who were about to pounce on Crook's outnumbered column. After warning Crook that he was riding into a trap, the Shoshones and the Crows launched a counter-charge that disrupted the Sioux long enough for Crook to extricate his men with the loss of only 57 killed or wounded. Eight days afterward, less than 20 miles to the northwest, Custer led his men to the slaughter along the Little Bighorn. Two years later, in 1878, Washakie's warriors helped Colonel Ranald S. Mackenzie track down the great Cheyenne war leader Dull Knife and his band in the Bighorn Mountains. By the following spring, Sitting Bull and his followers had fled to Canada, and Crazy Horse, Gall, and the other Sioux war chiefs had given themselves up.

Washington honored Washakie for his loyal service. Camp Brown was renamed Fort Washakie, and President Grant sent an official to present the old chief with a beautifully crafted saddle. Washakie was deeply touched. When the time came for him to speak, he uttered the words for which he is most remembered. "When a favor is shown a white man, he feels it in his head, and his tongue speaks," Washakie said with great emotion. "When a kindness is shown to an Indian, he feels it in his heart, and the heart has no tongue. I have spoken."

One of the last prominent war chiefs of the West, Quanah Parker, shown in a photograph taken about 1895, led swift-riding Comanches in raids on white settlers and the U.S. Army in a desperate attempt to maintain the traditional no-madic, hunting life and to stave off con-finement to reserva-tions. Parker later became a peacetime leader of his tribe.

A Comanche painting on deerskin portrays the ill-fated Indian attack in 1874 on heavily armed whites holed up near Adobe Walls in Texas. At bottom right, Quanah Parker uses a lance to impale an enemy through the cover on a wagon; the clouds of gun smoke around the building indicate the density of the defenders' long-range rifle fire.

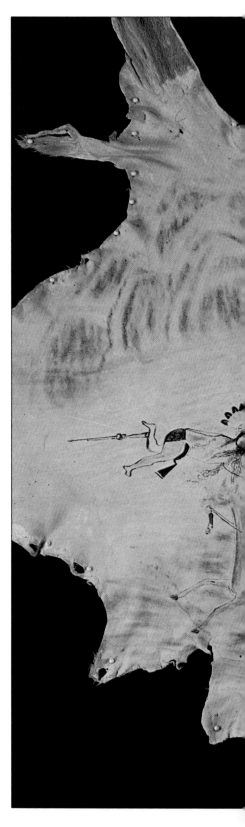

But soon afterward, Washington dealt Washakie a cruel blow. Eager to scatter the coalition of tribes that had so ferociously defended their homelands, the government ordered that the hostile Sioux, Cheyenne, and Arapaho bands be dispersed to widely separated reservations. The Sioux went to the Dakotas, the Cheyenne to Indian Territory, or present-day Oklahoma. The Arapaho—"enemies of the Shoshone since the birth of the oldest man," in Washakie's angry words—were inexplicably dumped onto the Shoshone Wind River Reservation. There they have remained to this day, despite Shoshone and Arapaho protests. In 1938, long after Washakie's death, the government finally agreed to compensate the Shoshone for giving away part of their land to one of their bitterest foes.

On the dry Texas plains 1,000 miles south of Washakie's beloved Wind River valley lived the proud and powerful Comanche. During the 1700s, these Uto-Aztecan speaking people broke off from their Shoshone relatives and migrated southward along the eastern face of the Rocky Mountains. At some point during their travels, they incorporated the horse into their culture and, within a century, became known far and wide for their skill at horse breeding. A single warrior sometimes owned as many as 250 horses. Astride their mounts, the Comanche and their Kiowa allies controlled a vast territory, including most of Texas, and parts of Oklahoma, Kansas, Colorado, and New Mexico. They often ventured several hundred miles into Mexico to seize horses, captives, and other booty.

After Texas won its independence in 1836 and settlers began to enter the region, the Comanche directed most of their raiding against the Texans. In proportion to their numbers—they probably never totaled more than a few thousand, although estimates range higher—the Comanche are thought to have killed more whites than any other tribe. Indeed, so fearsome was their reputation that even the Apache stayed clear of them.

Comanche society was organized loosely into a dozen or so autonomous bands. Each band had several leaders, a principal chief, and many noted warriors, any of whom could lead a war party. The number of people in each band fluctuated. Not infrequently, families transferred their allegiance from one band to another, depending upon the success of a band's hunting and raiding.

In the late 1840s or early 1850s in a region of west Texas known as the Staked Plain, a boy was born who would grow up to lead the Comanche in their final struggle against the whites. The boy's father was Peta Nocone, leader of one of the Comanche bands; his mother, a white

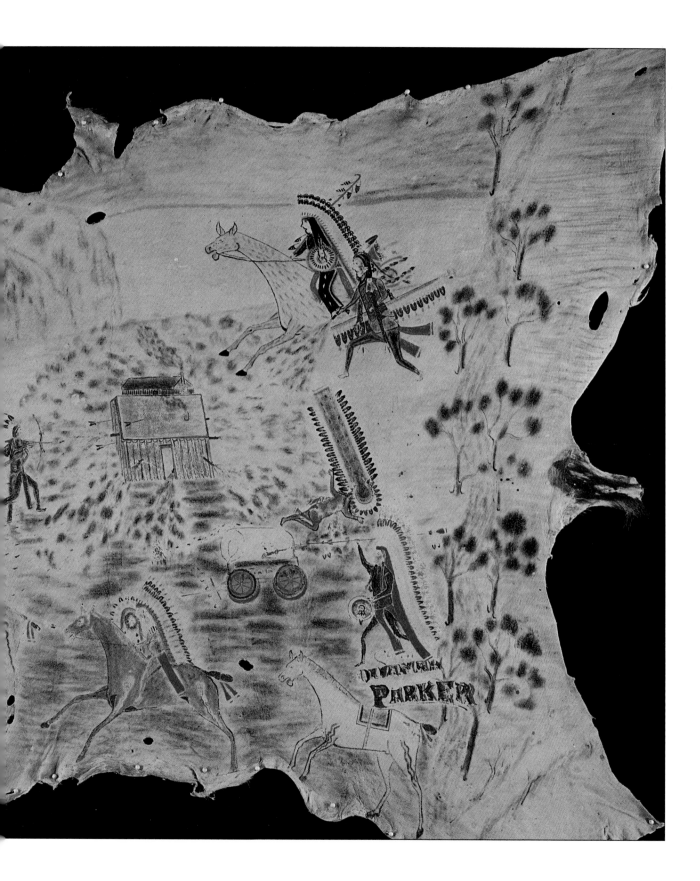

captive named Cynthia Ann Parker. According to some accounts, she had been captured at the age of nine by Caddo Indians and sold to the Comanche. Other stories relate that the Comanche abducted her from a Texas frontier homestead after murdering her parents.

The boy, named Quanah, spent his childhood on the vast, grassy plains. With other children, he engaged in rough sports and shot blue quail and prairie chickens with rifle and bow and arrow. He also learned to ride, practicing until he acquired the hallmark skill of a Comanche warrior: Secured only by a loop braided into the horse's mane, he was able to slip under the neck of his mount and let fly an arrow or a bullet.

The idyll of childhood came to an abrupt halt when Quanah was in his teens. That autumn of 1860, his family's band was camped on the Pease River in northern Texas, hunting buffalo. Spread out near a clear stream, with a ridge of clay cliffs to shelter them from the wind, the group was wholly unaware that a force of Texas Rangers was rapidly closing in. Suddenly the troopers struck, firing wildly. In the ensuing melee, Quanah's mother and little sister, Prairie Flower, were captured by the rangers; eventually they were recognized and returned to the Parker family. But within a few years, the child died of disease; and Cynthia Ann, who considered herself Comanche, starved herself to death in grief. The fate of Quanah's father is uncertain. By some accounts, he was killed by the rangers. Other stories state that he survived the battle only to die the next spring from a wound suffered in a raid. Whichever report is correct, an essential fact remained: Quanah had lost both his parents and was left to fend for himself. In later years, he recalled the depth of the sorrow he felt at their loss and admitted that it had haunted him all of his life.

Members of a Comanche peyote society (top), including Quanah Parker (seated, second from left) and a "roadman," or peyote priest, are shown on the morning after the ritualistic ingestion of the cactus-derived, hallucinogenic drug. The peyote religion, which came to tribes in the United States from Mexico, helped to induce the visions that have always been central to the spiritual experience of the Plains Indians.

Quanah drifted from one Comanche band to another. His proficiency as a horseman and warrior became legendary, and soon he was adopted by the Quahada, a hard-riding band who roved the Staked Plain region of west Texas. Quanah dedicated himself to avenging the loss of his parents. Quahada raids were notorious. A group of warriors would hide in the mountains beyond a ranch, then dart down, stampeding livestock and stealing horses. No white was spared. Those who were not killed were taken prisoner, to be held for ransom or adopted into the band.

In 1867 the U.S. government decided to put an end to the depredations. That autumn, a summons was sent to all the Indians in the region to gather for a huge council on Medicine Lodge Creek in southern Kansas. More than 4,000 Kiowas, Apaches, and Comanches responded. The government officials presented their terms. The violence must stop. All Indians must move to a reservation in the southern part of present-day Oklahoma, where they would learn to till the soil. For a time, the Indians would be allowed hunting privileges farther afield, but eventually they were expected to make their living as farmers.

Ten Bears, of the Yamparika band, spoke for the Comanche. "I was born on the prairie where the wind blew free, and there was nothing to break the light of the sun. I lived like my fathers before me, and like them, I lived happily," he explained. "Why do you ask us to leave the rivers, and the sun, and the wind, and live in houses? Do not ask us to give up the buffalo for the sheep."

But many of the chiefs present at the council signed the Medicine Lodge Treaty. Like other Indians of the day, they could not fathom a document that ordered them to surrender their lands and way of life forever and did not realize the consequences of their compliance. Enticed by gifts and the prospect of annuities, they scribbled their marks on the scrap of paper. When Quanah learned of the treaty, he was bitter. "My band is not going to live on a reservation," he asserted. "The Quahada are warriors."

For the next eight years, Quanah led the Quahada in a frenzy of looting and killing. Up and down the state, the band assaulted ranches, wagon trains, and cattle drives. As the years passed, other Comanches trickled onto the reservation, but the Quahada held out. Like-minded warriors joined them—Kiowas, Apaches, and others. The band constituted an impressive force. Well armed and mounted on sleek ponies, they could ride as far as 80 miles a day and still be ready for a fight.

When the U.S. Army tried to halt the Quahada rebellion, they failed, defeated by rough terrain, harsh weather, and the powerful resolve of a desperate people. A captain who survived a clash with the Quahada de-scribed their leader: Naked to the waist, the youthful warrior Quanah sat astride a black mustang and wielded a six-shooter. His face was smeared with war paint, and he wore the eagle-feathered bonnet of a chief.

In 1874 the Comanche decided to take revenge on the buffalo hunt-ers, who were exterminating the great beasts. The sight of rotting car-casses dotting the landscape so outraged the Indians that warriors both on and off the reservation answered a call to council. They met on the north fork of the Red River in the Texas Panhandle. There a medicine man named Eschiti told them he had a sacred war paint that offered pro-tection from the white man's powerful buffalo guns. At the close of the assembly, Quanah gathered a force of several hundred warriors, mostly Comanche and Cheyenne. Their target would be a trading post used by the hunters near the site of an old fort, Adobe Walls, in north Texas.

The trading post consisted of a saloon, a blacksmith shop, and two stores, all crudely but soundly fashioned from logs and sod. On the June day when Quanah attacked, there were 28 men and one woman inside the buildings. The Indians quickly killed two hunters and a large dog who were sleeping outside under a wagon. But their success ended there. Al-though the attackers poured fire into every window and gap in the walls of the buildings, they were repelled time and again by the deadly marks-manship of the buffalo hunters. Even before the first charge ended, a doz-en warriors had been hit. Quanah himself was stunned by a bullet that ricocheted off a rock and struck his shoulder.

The Comanches laid siege to the trading post, and on the third day, Quanah and a group of warriors rode up onto a butte to review the situ-ation. From where they were standing, the clump of buildings looked tiny. The Indians suddenly noticed a puff of bluish smoke curling in the air. Next there was a loud boom, and one of the warriors fell from his pony, pierced by a bullet fired from almost a mile away. Many years later, one Comanche who had been with Quanah at Adobe Walls recalled the event. "We lost the fight," he admitted sadly. "The buffalo hunters were too much for us. They stood behind Adobe Walls with telescopes on their ri-fles. Sometimes we would be standing way off, resting, and their guns would kill our horses." The medicine of the shaman Eschiti had failed.

Abandoning the siege, Quanah gathered his troops and led them back to the Staked Plain, where they managed to survive a parching drought. Meanwhile, the U.S. Army put out the word that any Indian found off the reservation would be treated as hostile. Then the Americans

Stars decorate the roof of the 12-room ranch house built for Quanah Parker by cattleman Burk Burnett on the Co-manche reservation. After he gave up fighting at about the age of 30, the shrewd Parker—who learned both Eng-lish and Spanish— became a successful rancher and promi-nent civil figure.

mustered six columns of troops and marched them against the Quahada from different directions. For months the army scoured the countryside, burning every Indian village they found and forcing the evacuees onto the reservation. But Quanah remained free. "They have not found me," he boasted. "The white men will walk a long way through the heat and not find water. Their horses will die. If they come near one of our camps, we can go away, and they will tire themselves out trying to find us again."

Despite his brave words, even Quanah was alarmed about his prospects. His band had suffered a harsh winter, and they were tired and hungry. With the buffalo nearly extinct, the Indians were reduced to hunting small game and scavenging for wild plants. All the same, Quanah was loath to surrender. One day, however, he saw something that changed his mind. Seated on a hill outside camp, he spotted a wolf far below him. Slowly the animal turned and gazed at the young chief, a low moan rising from its throat. Then it trotted briskly away, heading east, in the direction of the reservation. The action of the lone wolf seemed to be an omen that Quanah could not ignore. Rising from the hillside, he returned to camp and mustered his band for the journey to the land of the white men.

On June 2, 1875, Quanah surrendered at Fort Sill, the army post on the Comanche reservation in southern Oklahoma. The Quahada were pale, thin, and ill from months of privation. The Americans herded the once-fearsome warriors into a stone corral and stripped them of their weapons and their ponies. The three-million-acre reservation was a well-watered landscape of rolling plains, in the purple shadow of the Wichita Mountains. It was breathtaking scenery, but it was not a home. The Quahada had never lived behind a fence. As if in a bad dream, Quanah and his warriors listened to the white men talk of farming, raising livestock, sending Comanche children to school.

Yet Quanah found the fortitude to adapt. Like Washakie, he may have perceived that his best hope lay in cooperation. Quanah had not been on the reservation long when he requested permission to visit the Parker family in east Texas. On his uncle's ranch, he slept in a bed under the same flowered quilt that had warmed his mother. He went with his uncle to the cotton fields and the milking barn. He watched his aunt churn cream into butter. The brief visit did not end Quanah's yearning for the open plain and the buffalo hunt, but upon his return, he committed himself to helping his people change. He added his mother's surname to his Indian name and, over the next three decades, guided the Comanche in their struggle to become a settled people.

On the reservation, all the Comanche bands accepted Quanah as their leader, and he became a liaison between Indians and whites. When three Comanches attacked a soldier, Quanah intervened, so the entire tribe would not be punished. When horse thieves preyed on Indian herds, he received permission from the reservation agent to track down the rustlers and recover the ponies. When there was resistance among the Comanche to serving on a police force or to sending children to school, he stood firm, insisting that his people adapt to the white ways. He became a school board trustee and a judge on a court hearing Indian issues.

In the late 1870s, cattle ranchers trespassed regularly on Comanche land, driving their herds to market across the reservation. When all efforts to fend off the ranchers failed, Quanah demanded payment in exchange for grazing rights. Before long, leasing range land became a lucrative Comanche business, netting the community tens of thousands of dollars annually. Twice a year, Quanah distributed the payments among the people. In the course of administering the leases, he became friends with many of the stockmen; in time they repaid the friendship by building him a spacious house where he lived with his wives and their many children.

Although he adopted many white ways, Quanah never lost his Comanche spirituality. On his journey to his mother's family, he had taken a side trip to Mexico, to visit another Parker relative. While there, he was gored by a bull. Feverish and weak, he accepted the ministrations of a local Indian healer, who treated him with peyote, the crown of a small cactus. The hallucinogenic medicine induced a trance in which all pain vanished and Quanah saw visions of grassy plains, clear streams, and vast herds of buffalo. In his reverie, Quanah saw his mother holding a baby and smiling. Then he slept. When he awoke, his fever had vanished.

Peyote, Quanah decided, was a gift to the Indians from the Great Spirit to compensate them for all their losses. When he left Mexico, he took a large bundle of the cactus crowns with him. Back home in Texas, he shared the plant with his friends, and word of its power spread. Over time, Indians developed rituals around its use that became incorporated into a formal pantribal religion, the Native American Church.

Near the end of his life, Quanah and a party of Comanches joined the cattleman Charles Goodnight for a hunt on his ranch near the Palo Duro Canyon. As the Indian and the white man stood on the canyon rim gazing across the spectacular landscape, memories of the past flooded over both of them. Goodnight later spoke of his feelings that day. "My heart was moved," the rancher recalled, "as I stood on land, once theirs, but now wrested from their hands."

It was during this period that Quanah succeeded in paying a last tribute to his white mother. For many years, Quanah had considered moving his mother's remains to the Comanche reservation. Finally, in 1910, he obtained permission from the Parker family. The federal government contributed $1,000 to the effort, most of it for a monument. Quanah chose a hilly mound for the grave site, and on a day in December, more than 1,000 people, including both Comanches and whites, gathered to watch him reinter his mother's bones. Quanah spoke in English of his deep feelings for the mother he had lost as a boy. Then he shared his hopes for the Comanche. "I want my people to learn the white man's way," he said, "to get an education and know work. My people may die today, tomorrow, or in 10 years. I want them to be ready like my mother."

Quanah also spoke of his wish to be buried next to his mother. Two months later, while on a short trip, he fell ill. By the time he arrived home, his fever was raging. Even peyote brought no relief. On February 23, 1911, Quanah Parker passed away. He went to his chosen grave site clad in the buckskin regalia of a Comanche chief. ✛

THE EMERGENCE OF A CHIEF CALLED PLENTY COUPS

As Indian leaders across North America struggled to comprehend and cope with the overwhelming changes imposed by white conquest in the mid-19th century, the Absaroka, or Crow, found divine guidance in the prophetic dream of a nine-year-old boy. The child, Bull Who Goes into the Wind, experienced his powerful vision one spring in the late 1850s, when the tribe's scattered bands assembled at the foot of Montana's Beartooth Range for their annual gathering.

"I could see countless buffalo, see their sharp horns thick as grass grows. I could smell their bodies and hear them snorting," he related many years later. "Out of a hole in the ground came the bulls and cows and calves without number. They spread wide and blackened the plains. Everywhere I looked, great herds of buffalo were going in every direction, and still others without number were pouring out." Then, without warning, the buffalo disappeared. "All were gone, all! There was not one in sight."

Guided by a spirit, the boy next saw a vast herd of strangely configured "spotted buffalo" grazing on the plains. Then he was shown a sightless old man sitting beside a stream, and finally a great forest engulfed in a raging storm. When the winds subsided, all that stood was a single tree sheltering a lone chickadee.

The meaning of the dream was clear to the spiritual leader Yellow Bear, who interpreted it in council. The buffalo represented the Indian way of life, soon to be replaced by the white man's way—represented by the "spotted buffalo," or cattle. The storm was the might of the white man; the trees that resisted it were the tribes of the Plains, fated to be uprooted and destroyed. "By listening as the chickadee listens, we may escape this and keep our lands," concluded Yellow Bear. "And the one tree that the four winds left standing after the fearful battle represents our own people."

To the deeply religious Crow, who understand dreams as agents of spiritual instruction, this vision lent moral weight to a pragmatic course they had been following since the early 1800s. Numbering perhaps 14,000 and surrounded by more powerful, aggressive enemies, the Crow had embraced white fur traders as allies in their persistent conflicts with the Sioux, Blackfeet, Cheyenne, and Arapaho. Over subsequent years, they responded to the whites' requests for military assistance, helping protect travelers on the Bozeman Trail, scouting for Custer, and fighting with Crook at the Battle of the Rosebud. Despite the provocation of repeated broken promises, the Crow, alone among all the Plains tribes, rarely pointed their weapons at the invaders they called the Yellow Eyes.

The boy whose dream was instrumental in setting that policy grew during those turbulent years into a courageous and honored warrior. Acquiring the name Plenty Coups, he eventually rose to the rank of chief, emerging as a leader whose forceful advocacy of change brought him fame in the wide world and made him a figure of controversy among his own people.

"I have tried all my life to be just, even to those who have taken away our old life," said Plenty Coups at age 80, some 20 years after this photograph was taken. "My whole thought is of my people. I want them to be healthy, to become again the race they have been. I want them to learn all they can from the white man; because he is here to stay and they must live with him forever."

THE POWER OF A DREAM

Just as it forecast the fate of his people, Plenty Coups's dream showed the direction his life would take, even the site of his future home. It also revealed the identity of his own spiritual helper, whose example would govern his life-long conduct—the chickadee, known for its wisdom and ability to listen.

To the Crow, such revelations were paramount in determining the supernatural personal power essential to success in all endeavors. Medicine bundles, such as those owned by Plenty Coups and pictured here, contained the holy objects—known only to their owners—that embodied that power.

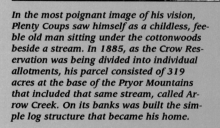

In the most poignant image of his vision, Plenty Coups saw himself as a childless, feeble old man sitting under the cottonwoods beside a stream. In 1885, as the Crow Reservation was being divided into individual allotments, his parcel consisted of 319 acres at the base of the Pryor Mountains that included that same stream, called Arrow Creek. On its banks was built the simple log structure that became his home.

One of Plenty Coups's medicine bundles was a cloth-wrapped pipestem—the sacred part of the pipe whose smoke placated the heavenly powers during the rituals of the Crow Medicine Pipe Society.

Plenty Coups derived his power from the secret items in his personal medicine bundle, kept in a painted rawhide case.

Sacred rock bundles like Plenty Coups's were seen as immutable manifestations of spiritual power, and thus a source of great strength.

Plenty Coups's Sacred Tobacco Society rattle is typical of those used by that group's ritual leaders. The rattle is made of two pieces of hide sewn around a short stick.

Plenty Coups's beaded sacred bundle attached to a neck thong. It may have held tobacco seeds, conduits of the Great Spirit's power.

THE SWIFT RISE OF A YOUNG WARRIOR

Plenty Coups belonged to the last generation of Indians to come of age as free men and to earn the rank of chief through acts of bravery. "A boy never wished to be a man more than I," he said of his ambitions. "How I wished to count coup, to wear an eagle's feather in my hair, to sit in council."

Fueled by the dreamed revelation that he would have no children of his own, but be father to all the Crow peoples, Plenty Coups rose quickly, proving himself in battle. He became chief of one of the largest of his tribe's bands when he was still in his thirties. In 1876 he was one of the leaders of the combined Crow-Shoshone force credited with saving General George Crook from defeat by the Sioux in the Battle of the Rosebud. "The soldier-chiefs will not forget that the Crows came to their aid," the chief promised his warriors.

The most striking badge of Plenty Coups's status was his war bonnet with its multitude of eagle feathers, indicating his wealth. The black-tipped ermine tails designated his rank as chief.

Still youthful-looking in his fifties, Plenty Coups holds some of the accouterments of his vanished life as a Plains fighter: his medicine pipe, the Pipe Holder's bag traditionally carried by war leaders, and a mirror—a device of great value to many warriors.

The chief's hollow bison horn, with a leather thong attached for carrying, served as a water cup from which the drinker might also imbibe the strength of the buffalo.

Bell Rock, a highly regarded older chief, gave his brother-in-law Plenty Coups this medicine bundle to confer some of his own good fortune on the younger man.

Plenty Coups's personal pipe is carved from soft red catlinite, the traditional sacred pipestone.

Two leather pouches and a dish-shaped hide disk held the paint that Plenty Coups applied to his face when he was preparing for battle.

The wing tip of a golden eagle was bound in a decorative handle to create Plenty Coups's eagle-feather fan—a badge of distinction at tribal gatherings.

LIVING THE WHITE MAN'S WAY

By the middle of the 1880s, the Crow Indians had moved to their reservation in the Yellowstone Valley of Montana, and Plenty Coups was eking out a living as a rancher, a farmer, and the proprietor of a small general store. He sold apples from his orchard, exhibited prize potatoes at Yellowstone County agricultural fairs, and was made an honorary member of the Billings Kiwanis Club.

Yet despite his seeming acceptance of white ways, the former warrior inwardly grieved for the lost past. As an old man, relating his life story to a biographer, he declined to discuss the decades after the passing of the buffalo—his refusal an eloquent comment on the desolation of reservation life. "When the buffalo went away, the hearts of my people fell to the ground, and they could not lift them up again. After this, nothing happened."

In 1928, inspired by a visit to Mount Vernon, Plenty Coups deeded his store (above), his house, and 40 acres to the government for a public park. "This spot was shown me in my great medicine dream," he explained. "I want my people to possess it forever, just as white men own and keep the home of their great chief, George Washington."

A small cylinder held the crayons that Plenty Coups used to color the pictograph ledger, shown at right, in which he kept his store accounts.

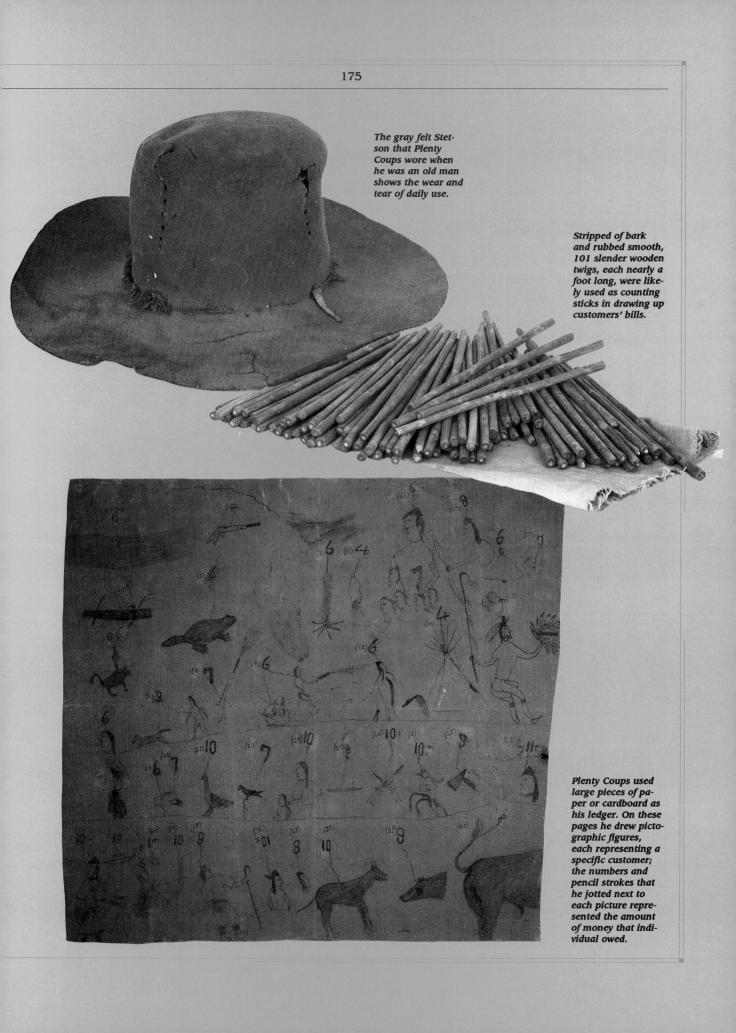

The gray felt Stetson that Plenty Coups wore when he was an old man shows the wear and tear of daily use.

Stripped of bark and rubbed smooth, 101 slender wooden twigs, each nearly a foot long, were likely used as counting sticks in drawing up customers' bills.

Plenty Coups used large pieces of paper or cardboard as his ledger. On these pages he drew pictographic figures, each representing a specific customer; the numbers and pencil strokes that he jotted next to each picture represented the amount of money that individual owed.

Plenty Coups, seated second from right, made his first trip to Washington in 1880 as part of a Crow delegation. Years later, his experience and friendship with whites helped keep the Crow Reservation closed to homesteading (although the Indians were allowed to sell or lease land to whites).

DIPLOMAT AND ELDER STATESMAN

Thanks in large part to their early decision to ally themselves with the whites, the Crow peoples largely avoided the military punishment that was meted out to their deadly enemies. The Crow were among the few Native American nations to remain intact on one reservation, having retained a portion of their ancestral homeland.

The humiliating restraints of reservation life, however, along with the steady whittling away of their land (from the original 38.8 million acres established by treaty in 1851 to its present 2.2 million acres), provoked anger among many younger Crows

and resentment toward leaders such as Plenty Coups, who continued to counsel cooperation with the officials in Washington and even supported hated white policies such as the compulsory education of Indian children in government and mission schools.

Unfortunately for his reputation among other Native Americans, Plenty Coups's willingness to negotiate was responsible for creating the image of a compliant leader whose function was limited to appearances at public ceremonies. The popular press sometimes erroneously styled him the sole chief of the Crow Nation, or even "Chief of all

the Tribes of the Northwest"—embarrassing titles he disavowed.

Despite all that, Plenty Coups continued to defend the rights of his community and expressed no second thoughts about his lifelong conciliatory policy toward the whites, maintaining that it helped his people repel the most drastic inroads on their freedom. In addition, he openly rejoiced in the fact that the Crow Nation had secured a reservation in their own country. "When I think back, my heart sings because we acted as we did," he declared shortly before his death in 1932. "It was the only way open to us."

"Presented by Albert first Prince of Monaco to Chief Plenty Coos on the occasion of his first meeting with an Indian Chief," reads a plaque on the 1895 Winchester rifle Plenty Coups received in 1913 from the monarch.

One of the world leaders Plenty Coups counted among his friends, French field marshal Ferdinand Foch (left, front) visited the Crow Reservation in 1921 and was made a ceremonial member of the tribe.

Present at Woodrow Wilson's first inaugural in 1913, Plenty Coups took home a bronze medal struck to commemorate the occasion.

Plenty Coups laid his war bonnet and coup stick on the casket at the 1921 dedication of the Tomb of the Unknowns. Proud of the Crow soldiers who fought in World War I, he later vowed that "if ever the hands of my own people hold the rope that keeps this country's flag high in the air, it will never come down."

178

ACKNOWLEDGMENTS

The editors wish to thank the following individuals and institutions for their valuable assistance.

In Canada: Alberta—Seema Bharadia, Glenbow Museum, Calgary. British Columbia—Dan Savard, Royal British Columbia Museum, Victoria. Ontario—Bob Garcia, Fort Malden National Historic Site, Amherstburg.
In Germany: Stuttgart—Ursula Didoni, Linden Museum.
In Switzerland: Bern—Historisches Museum.
In the United States:
Arizona: Tucson—Theodore R. Bundy, Arizona State Museum; Heather Hatch, Arizona Historical Society.

California: Arcata—Erich Schimps, Humboldt State University. Eureka—Amos Tripp, Maria Tripp. Santa Cruz—Triloki Pandey, University of California. Trinidad—Jerome J. Simone, United Indian Health Service.
Connecticut: Storrs—James Faris, University of Connecticut.
Illinois: Rock Island—Elizabeth Carvey-Stewart, Black Hawk State Historic Site.
Iowa: Iowa City—George D. Schrimper, University of Iowa Museum of Natural History; Peter Stevenson, University of Iowa Museum of Art.
Missouri: Kansas City—Julie Mattson, Denise Morrison, Kansas City Museum.
Montana: Browning—Darrell Robes Kipp, Piegan Institute. Pryor—Rich Pittsley, Chief Plenty Coups State Park.

New Mexico: Santa Fe—Keith Basso, University of New Mexico; Laura Holt, Museum of New Mexico.
North Dakota: Bismarck—Todd Strand, State Historical Society of North Dakota.
Oklahoma: Fort Sill-Towana Spivey, Fort Sill Museum.
Washington, D.C.: David C. Burgevin, Office of Printing and Photographic Services, Smithsonian Insitution; Paula Fleming, James Harwood and the Archives Staff, National Anthropological Archives, Smithsonian Institution; William Perry, The National Geographic Society; Felicia Pickering, National Museum of Natural History, Smithsonian Institution.
Washington State: Seattle—Rebecca Andrews, Bill Holm, The Burke Museum, University of Washington; Jay Miller; Sari Ott, Stan Shockey, University of Washington.

BIBLIOGRAPHY

BOOKS
Andrist, Ralph K., *The Long Death: The Last Days of the Plains Indian.* New York: MacMillan, 1964.
Ball, Eve, *In the Days of Victorio: Recollections of a Warm Springs Apache.* Tucson: University of Arizona Press, 1970.
Ball, Eve, Nora Henn, and Lynda A. Sánchez, *Indeh: An Apache Odyssey.* Norman: University of Oklahoma Press, 1988.
Barrett, S. M., ed., *Geronimo: His Own Story.* New York: E. P. Dutton, 1970.
Basso, Keith H., E. W. Jernigan, and W. B. Kessell, eds., *Western Apache Raiding and Warfare: From the Notes of Grenville Goodwin.* Tucson: University of Arizona Press, 1971.
Bourke, John G., *On the Border with Crook.* Lincoln: University of Nebraska Press, 1971.
Brandon, William, *Indians.* Boston: Houghton Mifflin, 1989.
Brown, Dee, *Bury My Heart at Wounded Knee: An Indian History of the American West.* New York: Henry Holt, 1991.
Capps, Benjamin, and the Editors of Time-Life Books, *The Great Chiefs* (The Old West series). Alexandria, Va.: Time-Life Books, 1975.
Connell, Evan S., *Son of the Morning Star.* New York: Harper Perennial, 1991.
D'Azevedo, Warren L., ed., *Great Basin.* Vol. 11 of *Handbook of North American Indians.* Washington, D.C.: Smithsonian Institution, 1986.
Debo, Angie, *Geronimo: The Man, His Time, His Place.* Norman: University of Oklahoma Press, 1976.
Dempsey, Hugh A., *Treasures of the Glenbow Museum.* Calgary, Alberta: Glenbow-Alberta Institute, 1991.

Densmore, Frances, *Chippewa Customs.* St. Paul: Minnesota Historical Society Press, 1979.
Dowd, Gregory Evans, *A Spirited Resistance: The North American Indian Struggle for Unity, 1745-1815.* Baltimore: Johns Hopkins University Press, 1992.
Driver, Harold E., *Indians of North America.* Chicago: University of Chicago Press, 1969.
Dutton, Bertha P., *American Indians of the Southwest.* Albuquerque: University of New Mexico Press, 1983.
Eastman, Charles A., *Indian Heroes and Great Chieftains.* Lincoln: University of Nebraska Press, 1991 (reprint of 1918 edition).
Edmunds, R. David, *Tecumseh and the Quest for Indian Leadership.* Ed. by Oscar Handlin. Boston: Little, Brown, 1984.
Emanuels, George, *California Indians: An Illustrated Guide.* Walnut Creek, Calif.: Diablo Books, 1991.
The Encyclopedia of Collectibles: Matchsafes to Nursing Bottles, by the Editors of Time-Life Books. Alexandria, Va.: Time-Life Books, 1979.
Foster, Morris W., *Being Comanche: A Social History of an American Indian Community.* Tucson: University of Arizona Press, 1991.
Freedman, Russell, *Indian Chiefs.* New York: Holiday House, 1987.
Gilbert, Bil, *God Gave Us This Country: Tekamthi and the First American Civil War.* New York: Atheneum, 1989.
Goble, Paul, and Dorothy Goble, *Brave Eagle's Account of the Fetterman Fight, 21 December 1866.* New York: Pantheon Books, 1972.
Grinnell, George Bird, *The Cheyenne Indians: Their History and Ways of Life.* Lincoln: University of Nebraska Press, 1972 (reprint of 1923 edition).
Hagan, William T., *United States-Comanche Relations: The Reservation Years.* Norman: University

of Oklahoma Press, 1990.
Haley, James L., *Apaches: A History and Culture Portrait.* Garden City, N.Y.: Doubleday, 1981.
Hebard, Grace Raymond, *Washakie: An Account of Indian Resistance of the Covered Wagon and Union Pacific Railroad Invasions of Their Territory.* Cleveland: Arthur H. Clark, 1930.
Higueras, María Dolores, *NW Coast of America: Iconographic Album of the Malaspina Expedition.* Madrid: Museo Naval y Lunwerg Editores, 1991.
Hodge, Frederick Webb, ed., *Handbook of American Indians North of Mexico.* Parts I and II. New York: Rowman and Littlefield, 1971.
Holm, Bill:
Smoky-Top: The Art and Times of Willie Seaweed. Seattle: University of Washington Press, 1983.
Spirit and Ancestor: A Century of Northwest Coast Indian Art at the Burke Museum. Seattle: Thomas Burke Memorial Washington State Museum, 1987.
Hook, Jason, *American Indian Warrior Chiefs: Tecumseh, Crazy Horse, Chief Joseph, Geronimo.* Poole, U.K.: Firebird Books, 1990.
Horan, James D., *The McKenney-Hall Portrait Gallery of American Indians.* New York: Bramhall House, 1986.
Hoxie, Frederick E., "Building a Future on the Past," in *Indian Leadership.* Ed. by Walter L. Williams. Manhattan, Kans.: Sunflower University Press, 1984.
Hyde, George E., *Red Cloud's Folk: A History of the Oglala Sioux Indians.* Norman: University of Oklahoma Press, 1976.
Jackson, Clyde L., and Grace Jackson, *Quanah Parker, Last Chief of the Comanches: A Study in Southwestern Frontier History.* New York: Exposition Press, 1963.
Jackson, Donald, ed., *Black Hawk: An Autobiogra-*

phy. Champaign: University of Illinois Press, 1990.

Jacobs, Wilbur R., *Dispossessing the American Indian: Indians and Whites on the Colonial Frontier*. Norman: University of Oklahoma Press, 1985.

Josephy, Alvin M., Jr.:

The Indian Heritage of America. Boston: Houghton Mifflin, 1991.

The Nez Perce Indians and the Opening of the Northwest. New Haven, Conn.: Yale University, 1965.

The Patriot Chiefs: A Chronicle of American Indian Leadership. New York: The Viking Press, 1961.

Josephy, Alvin M., Jr., ed., *The American Heritage Book of Indians*. New York: American Heritage Publishing, 1961.

Linderman, Frank B., *American: The Life Story of a Great Indian*. New York: John Day, 1930.

Lossing, Benson J., *The Pictorial Fieldbook of the War of 1812*. Somersworth: New Hampshire Publishing, 1976 (reprint of 1869 edition).

Lowie, Robert H., *The Crow Indians*. Lincoln: University of Nebraska Press, 1983.

McMillan, Alan D., *Native Peoples and Cultures of Canada: An Anthropological Overview*. Vancouver: Douglas & McIntyre, 1988.

Melody, Michael E., *The Apache*. New York: Chelsea House Publishers, 1989.

Moquin, Wayne, and Charles Van Doren, eds., *Great Documents in American Indian History*. New York: Praeger Publishers, 1973.

Nabokov, Peter, ed., *Native American Testimony: A Chronicle of Indian-White Relations from Prophecy to the Present, 1492-1992*. New York: Viking Penguin, 1991.

The Native Americans: The Indigenous People of North America. New York: Smithmark Publishers, 1991.

Neihardt, John G., *Black Elk Speaks: Being the Life Story of a Holy Man of the Ogalala Sioux*. New York: William Morrow, 1932.

The New World, Vol. 1: Prehistory to 1774, by the Editors of Life (The Life History of the United States series). New York: Time-Life Books, 1963.

Nichols, Roger L., *Black Hawk and the Warrior's Path*. Arlington Heights, Ill.: Harlan Davidson, 1992.

Olson, James C., *Red Cloud and the Sioux Problem*. Lincoln: University of Nebraska Press, 1965.

Opler, Morris Edward, *An Apache Life-Way: The Economic, Social, and Religious Institutions of the Chiricahua Indians*. New York: Cooper Square Publishers, 1965.

Ourada, Patricia K., *The Menominee*. New York: Chelsea House Publishers, 1990.

Parker, Arthur C., *The Life of General Ely S. Parker, Last Grand Sachem of the Iroquois and General Grant's Military Secretary*. Buffalo: Buffalo Historical Society, 1919.

Prucha, Francis Paul, *Indian Peace Medals in American History*. Madison: State Historical Society of Wisconsin, 1971.

Reynolds, Charles R., Jr., ed., *American Indian Portraits from the Wanamaker Expedition of 1913*. Brattleboro, Vt.: Stephen Greene Press, 1971.

Ritzenthaler, Robert E., and Pat Ritzenthaler, *The Woodland Indians of the Western Great Lakes*. Prospect Heights, Ill.: Waveland Press, 1991.

Rollings, Willard H., *The Comanche*. New York: Chelsea House Publishers, 1989.

Skarsten, M. O., *Those Remarkable People: The Dakotas and Lakotas*. N.p., 1981.

Sneve, Virginia Driving Hawk, *They Led a Nation*. Sioux Falls, S. Dak.: Brevet Press, 1975.

Standing Bear, Luther:

Land of the Spotted Eagle. Lincoln: University of Nebraska Press, 1978.

My People the Sioux. Ed. by E. A. Brininstool. Lincoln: University of Nebraska Press, 1975.

Story of the Great American West. Pleasantville, N.Y.: Reader's Digest Association, 1977.

Sugden, John, *Tecumseh's Last Stand*. Norman: University of Oklahoma Press, 1985.

Sweeney, Edwin R., *Cochise: Chiricahua Apache Chief*. Norman: University of Oklahoma Press, 1991.

Tanner, Helen Hornbeck, *The Ojibwa*. New York: Chelsea House Publishers, 1992.

Tanner, Helen Hornbeck, ed., *Atlas of Great Lakes Indian History*. Norman: University of Oklahoma Press, 1987.

Thornton, Russell, *American Indian Holocaust and Survival: A Population History Since 1492*. Norman: University of Oklahoma Press, 1987.

Thrapp, Dan L.:

The Conquest of Apacheria. Norman: University of Oklahoma Press, 1967.

Victorio and the Mimbres Apaches. Norman: University of Oklahoma Press, 1974.

Tilghman, Zoe A., *Quanah: The Eagle of the Comanches*. Oklahoma City: Harlow Publishing, 1938.

Treasures. Hull, Quebec: Canadian Museum of Civilization, 1988.

Trenholm, Virginia Cole, and Maurine Carley, *The Shoshonis: Sentinels of the Rockies*. Norman: University of Oklahoma Press, 1964.

Trigger, Bruce G., ed., *Northeast*. Vol. 15 of *Handbook of North American Indians*. Washington, D.C.: Smithsonian Institution, 1978.

Underhill, Ruth Murray, *Red Man's America: A History of Indians in the United States*. Chicago: University of Chicago Press, 1971.

Utley, Robert M., *The Indian Frontier of the American West, 1846-1890*. Albuquerque: University of New Mexico Press, 1984.

Utley, Robert M., and Wilcomb E. Washburn, *The American Heritage History of the Indian Wars*. New York: American Heritage Publishing, 1982.

Viola, Herman J.:

Diplomats in Buckskins: A History of Indian Delegations in Washington City. Washington, D.C.: Smithsonian Institution Press, 1981.

The Indian Legacy of Charles Bird King. Washington, D.C.: Smithsonian Institution Press, 1976.

Thomas L. McKenney, Architect of America's Early Indian Policy: 1816-1830. Chicago: Swallow Press, 1974.

Waldman, Carl:

Atlas of the North American Indian. New York: Facts On File Publications, 1985.

Encyclopedia of Native American Tribes. New York: Facts On File Publications, 1988.

Who Was Who in Native American History: Indians and Non-Indians from Early Contacts through 1900. New York: Facts On File Publications, 1990.

Washburn, Wilcomb E., ed., *History of Indian-White Relations*. Vol. 4 of *Handbook of North American Indians*. Washington, D.C.: Smithsonian Institution, 1988.

Weinstein-Farson, Laurie, *The Wampanoag*. New York: Chelsea House Publishers, 1989.

White, Richard, *The Middle Ground: Indians, Empires, and Republics in the Great Lakes Region, 1650-1815*. New York: Cambridge University Press, 1991.

Wilfong, Cheryl, *Following the Nez Perce Trail: A Guide to the Nee-Me-Poo National Historic Trail with Eyewitness Accounts*. Corvallis: Oregon State University Press, 1990.

Worcester, Donald E., *The Apaches: Eagles of the Southwest*. Norman: University of Oklahoma Press, 1979.

Wright, Robin K., ed., *A Time of Gathering: Native Heritage in Washington State*. Seattle: Thomas Burke Memorial Washington State Museum, 1991.

Wunder, John R., *The Kiowa*. New York: Chelsea House Publishers, 1989.

Yenne, Bill, *The Encyclopedia of North American Indian Tribes: A Comprehensive Study of Tribes from the Abitibi to the Zuni*. New York: Arch Cape Press, 1986.

PERIODICALS

Fenton, William N., "Leadership in the Northeastern Woodlands of North America." *American Indian Quarterly*, Winter 1986.

Lindsay, G. Carroll, "The Treaty Pipe of the Delawares." *Antiques*, July 1958.

Mickelson, Gary E., "Notes on French Medals." *The Museum of the Fur Trade Quarterly*, Fall 1973.

"Photographing Delegates to an Indian Conference." *Frank Leslie's Illustrated Newspaper*, September 10, 1881.

Viola, Herman J.:

"Invitation to Washington." *The American West*, January 1972.

"Lincoln and the Indians." *Historical Bulletin*, State Historical Society of Wisconsin, Vol. 31, 1976.

OTHER PUBLICATIONS

Deaver, Sherri, and Kevin Jon Kooistra, "National Landmark Nomination Form for Chief Plenty Coups State Park." Grant proposal. Billings, Mont., 1991.

Hoxie, Frederick E., "Crow Leadership Amidst Reservation Oppression." Unpublished ms. Newberry Library, Chicago, 1991.

Lavender, David, *Fort Laramie and the Changing Frontier*. National Park Handbook No. 118. Washington, D.C., National Park Service, 1983.

Ledger Art of the Crow and Gros Ventre Indians: 1879-1897. Catalog. Billings, Mont., Yellowstone Art Center, 1985.

Maurer, Evan M., *Visions of the People: A Pictorial History of Plains Indian Life*. Catalog. Minneapolis, Minneapolis Institute of Arts, 1992.

Nez Perce Country. National Park Handbook No. 121. Washington, D.C., National Park Service, 1983.

Prucha, Francis Paul, *Peace and Friendship: Indian Peace Medals in the United States*. Catalog. Washington, D.C., Smithsonian Institution, 1985.

PICTURE CREDITS

The sources for the illustrations that appear in this book are listed below. Credits from left to right are separated by semicolons; from top to bottom they are separated by dashes.

Cover: State Historical Society of North Dakota. **6:** Courtesy Kansas City Museum–National Anthropological Archives (NAA), Smithsonian Institution, Washington, D.C., no. 270-A. **8:** Neg. no. 316906, photo by Rodman Wanamaker, courtesy Department of Library Services, American Museum of Natural History. **11:** Museo Naval, Madrid–Peabody Museum, Harvard University, photo by Hillel Burger, photo no. T708. **12:** Courtesy Bern Historical Museum, photo by Stefan Rebsamen–National Museum of American Art, Washington, D.C./Art Resource, New York. **14, 15:** Sy Seidman Collection, courtesy Culver Pictures; Larry Sherer, courtesy Department of Anthropology, Smithsonian Institution, Washington, D.C., no. 362061; Museum of the Fur Trade, Chadron, Nebraska. **16, 17:** © Tom Cawley. **18:** Ambrose Santiago, courtesy Steve Child–photo by Karen Furth, courtesy National Museum of the American Indian, Smithsonian Institution, Washington, D.C., no. 9/5210. **20, 21:** Library of Congress; Larry Sherer, courtesy Department of Anthropology, Smithsonian Institution, Washington, D.C., no. 5434–no. 5396. **23-25:** The Granger Collection. **26:** National Archives of Canada, Ottawa, Ontario. **27:** Culver Pictures. **29:** The Bettmann Archive. **30, 31:** The Board of Trustees of the National Museums and Galleries of Merseyside, Liverpool, England, courtesy Canadian Museum of Civilization, neg. no. S89-1740; Canadian Museum of Civilization, neg. no. S75-376 (2); neg. no. S75-357–neg. no. S75-514–neg. no. S75-523–neg. no. S75-357. **35:** Rare Books and Manuscripts Division, The New York Public Library, Astor, Lenox and Tilden Foundations. **36:** Werner Forman Archive/British Museum, London. **37:** Larry Sherer, courtesy Department of Anthropology, Smithsonian Institution, Washington, D.C., no. 203781; no. 360233A–Joslyn Art Museum, Omaha, Nebraska. **38:** National Museum of American Art, Washington, D.C./Art Resource, New York; State Historical Society of North Dakota–NAA, Smithsonian Institution, Washington, D.C., no. 427. **39:** The Paul Dyck Foundation, Rimrock, Arizona. **40:** Library of Congress; Peabody Museum, Harvard University, photo by Hillel Burger, photo no. T1223a–Humboldt State University. **41:** Phoebe Apperson Hearst Museum of Anthropology, University of California at Berkeley; Victor R. Boswell, © National Geographic Society, owned by the Phoebe Apperson Hearst Museum of Anthropology. **42:** State Historical Society of Iowa. **43:** Library of Congress, no. 307545; University of Iowa Museum of Natural History; Collection of Glenbow, Calgary, Alberta, AF 1872–NAA, Smithsonian Institution, Washington, D.C., no. 690A. **44:** Courtesy of the Thomas Burke Memorial Washington State Museum, catalog no. 2.5L46, photo by Eduardo Calderón. **45:** The Brooklyn Museum 05.588.7413, Museum Expedition 1905, Museum Collection Fund; courtesy of the Thomas Burke Memorial Washington State Museum, catalog no. 951, photo by Eduardo Calderón; courtesy of the Thomas Burke Memorial Washington State Museum, catalog no. 1-1443, photo by Eduardo Cal-

derón–courtesy of the Thomas Burke Memorial Washington State Museum, catalog no. 1-1436, photo by Eduardo Calderón. **46, 47:** Trans. no. 4571(2), photo by Lynton Gardiner, courtesy Department of Library Services, American Museum of Natural History; neg. no. 22861, courtesy Department of Library Services, American Museum of Natural History; Peabody Museum, Harvard University, photo by Hillel Burger, photo no. T1253–Royal British Columbia Museum, PN 2300-A. **48:** NAA, Smithsonian Institution, Washington, D.C., no. 49,389A–The Brooklyn Museum 30.797, Estate of Stewart Culin, Museum Purchase; trans. no. 4914(1), photo by J. Beckett, courtesy Department of Library Services, American Museum of Natural History. **49:** Seaver Center for Western History Research, Natural History Museum of Los Angeles County; Rare Books and Manuscripts Division, The New York Public Library, Astor, Lenox and Tilden Foundations. **50:** Field Museum of Natural History, neg. no. A-93851.1c. **52:** NAA, Smithsonian Institution, Washington, D.C., no. 794. **53:** Map by Maryland CartoGraphics, Inc. **56, 57:** Courtesy National Museum of the American Indian, Smithsonian Institution, Washington, D.C., no. 20811; Environment Canada, Parks Service/Fort Malden National Historic Site–Vern Harvey, Windsor, Ontario (2). **60, 61:** Ohio Historical Society. **62:** National Museum of American Art, Washington, D.C./Art Resource, New York. **64, 65:** Library of Congress. **67:** J. Lambert, National Archives of Canada, Ottawa, Ontario, C14488. **68:** Environment Canada, Parks Service/Fort Malden National Historic Site. **71:** The Warner Collection of Gulf States Paper Corporation, Tuscaloosa, Alabama. **72:** Gilcrease Institute of American History and Art, Tulsa, Oklahoma. **74:** Bob Motz, Citizens to Preserve Black Hawk Park Foundation, Rock Island, Illinois. **75:** Map by Maryland CartoGraphics, Inc. **76, 77:** Missouri Historical Society, photo by David Schultz; Hauberg Indian Museum, Black Hawk State Historic Site, administered by the Illinois Historic Preservation Agency–Ferrel Anderson, Black Hawk State Historic Site, Rock Island, Illinois. **78:** National Museum of American Art, Washington, D.C./Art Resource, New York. **79:** Rare Books and Manuscripts Division, The New York Public Library, Astor, Lenox and Tilden Foundations. **80:** National Museum of American Art, Washington, D.C./Art Resource, New York. **82, 83:** National Archives–Culver Pictures–NAA, Smithsonian Institution, Washington, D.C., no. 55942. **84, 85:** Courtesy Decorative and Industrial Arts Collection of the Chicago Historical Society–Library of Congress, USZ-62-4678; National Archives (2). **86, 87:** NAA, Smithsonian Institution, Washington, D.C., no. 3179c. **88, 89:** Charles H. Barstow Collection, Eastern Montana College, photographed by Michael Crummett (2); National Museum of American Art, Washington, D.C./Art Resource, New York; NAA, Smithsonian Institution, Washington, D.C., no. 48278; Musée de l'Homme, Paris, photo by J. Oster. **90, 91:** NAA, Smithsonian Institution, Washington, D.C., no. 2860-ZZ-21–no. 55300; Larry Sherer, courtesy Department of Anthropology, Smithsonian Institution, Washington, D.C., no. 128345; NAA, Smithsonian Institution, Washington, D.C., no. 3263-A–Larry Sherer, courtesy Museum of Natural History, Smithsonian Institution, Washington, D.C. **92:** Courtesy Museum of New Mexico, neg. no. 144740. **94, 95:**

NAA, Smithsonian Institution, Washington, D.C., no. 34011B. **97:** Map by Maryland CartoGraphics, Inc. **99:** Arizona State Museum, University of Arizona, photo by Helga Teiwes. **102, 103:** Bruce Dale, © National Geographic Society. **104:** Courtesy Arizona Historical Society, Tucson, neg. no. 929. **106, 107:** Henry Groskinsky, courtesy The American Numismatic Society, New York, except photo NAA, Smithsonian Institution, Washington, D.C., no. 3580-A. **110:** Courtesy Arizona Historical Society, Tucson, neg. no. 30371. **112, 113:** Bruce Dale, © National Geographic Society. **114, 115:** Paulus Leeser, courtesy Fort Sill Museum, Oklahoma, except photo C. S. Fly, courtesy Museum of New Mexico, neg. no. 2115. **116:** Collection of Glenbow, Calgary, Alberta, R37.928. **117:** Glenbow Archives, Calgary, Alberta, NA 5422-1. **119:** Courtesy Arizona Historical Society, Tucson, neg. no. 19796. **120:** Courtesy Arizona Historical Society, Tucson, neg. no. 30425. **121:** Fort Sill Museum, Oklahoma. **122, 123:** Courtesy of the National Park Service; map by Maryland CartoGraphics, Inc.–NAA, Smithsonian Institution, Washington, D.C., no. 2923A; no. 2922-A. **124, 125:** Haynes Foundation Collection, Montana Historical Society, Helena; David Jensen (2). **126, 127:** NAA, Smithsonian Institution, Washington, D.C., no. 2952-C; David Jensen. **128, 129:** Historical Photograph Collections, Washington State University Libraries; David Jensen (2). **130, 131:** David Jensen (2)–NAA, Smithsonian Institution, Washington, D.C., no. 2953A. **132-135:** David Jensen. **136:** Culver Pictures. **138, 139:** Buffalo Bill Historical Center, Cody, Wyoming/Adolph Spohr Collection, gift of Mr. Larry Sheerin. **143:** Map by Maryland CartoGraphics, Inc. **145:** Cumberland County Historical Society, Carlisle, Pennsylvania. **146, 147:** NAA, Smithsonian Institution, Washington, D.C., no. 56649; courtesy National Museum of the American Indian, Smithsonian Institution, Washington, D.C., no. 23/2202. **149:** Smithsonian Institution, Washington, D.C., no. 82-15200. **151:** American Heritage Center, University of Wyoming. **152, 153:** Wyoming Division of Tourism. **154, 155:** Haynes Foundation Collection, Montana Historical Society, Helena. **156, 157:** American Heritage Center, University of Wyoming. **159:** NAA, Smithsonian Institution, Washington, D.C., no. 56374. **160, 161:** Photo by Ruth Gartland. **162-165:** Fort Sill Museum, Oklahoma. **169:** Library of Congress, USZ62-98534. **170, 171:** Michael Crummett, courtesy Chief Plenty Coups State Park Museum, Pryor, Montana, except photos courtesy Chief Plenty Coups State Park Museum, Pryor, Montana. **172, 173:** Michael Crummett, courtesy Chief Plenty Coups State Park Museum, Pryor, Montana, except photo NAA, Smithsonian Institution, Washington, D.C., no. 42020A. **174:** Chief Plenty Coups State Park Museum, Pryor, Montana–Michael Crummett, courtesy Chief Plenty Coups State Park Museum, Pryor, Montana. **175:** Michael Crummett, courtesy Chief Plenty Coups State Park Museum, Pryor, Montana (2)–courtesy The Edward E. Ayer Collection, The Newberry Library, Chicago. **176, 177:** NAA, Smithsonian Institution, Washington, D.C., no. 49379; Michael Crummett, courtesy Chief Plenty Coups State Park Museum, Pryor, Montana–Chief Plenty Coups State Park Museum, Pryor, Montana; Michael Crummett, courtesy Chief Plenty Coups State Park Museum, Pryor, Montana–Chief Plenty Coups State Park Museum, Pryor, Montana.

INDEX